# EMPLOYEE MANAGEMENT

## and Customer Service
## in the Retail Industry

STOURBRIDGE
—COLLEGE—

## Hagley Road Centre

This book is to be returned on or before the last date stamped below.

20.3.08

# EMPLOYEE MANAGEMENT

## and Customer Service in the Retail Industry

## GARY HEIL

## CHRIS THOMAS

WILEY

JOHN WILEY & SONS, INC.

This book is printed on acid-free paper. ∞

Copyright © 2006 by John Wiley & Sons, Inc. All rights reserved.

Published by John Wiley & Sons, Inc., Hoboken, New Jersey
Published simultaneously in Canada

For general information on our other products and services or for technical support, please contact our Customer Care Department within the United States at (800) 762-2974, outside the United States at (317) 572-3993 or fax (317) 572-4002.

Wiley also publishes its books in a variety of electronic formats. Some content that appears in print may not be available in electronic books. For more information about Wiley products, visit our web site at www.wiley.com.

**Library of Congress Cataloging-in-Publication Data:**

ISBN-13: 978-0-471-72324-0
ISBN-10: 0-471-72324-X

Printed in the United States of America

10 9 8 7 6 5 4 3 2 1

# CONTENTS

# PREFACE

"By working faithfully eight hours a day, you may eventually get to be a boss and work 12 hours a day."

Robert Frost

It takes a sense of humor and a real work ethic to be in retail management nowadays, but it takes many other traits and skills as well. This book attempts to combine the psychology of dealing with employees and customers with the practical realities of managing a retail business—topics that, at times, seem at odds in the world of buying and selling merchandise.

The book is organized into 10 chapters and loosely follows a retail manager's natural progression from interviewing prospective employees to hiring the right ones, paying them fairly, and keeping them happy on the job. Happiness wasn't in the job description, you say? Perhaps not. But if a retailer expects employees to keep the customers happy, it follows that the employees should also be content on the job. Since about one-third of retail workers leave their jobs every year—the majority to go to work for a competitor—there is obviously room for improvement.

Chapter 1 begins with information about how to write a job description, a necessary precursor to advertising and hiring for a particular position. The processes of analyzing résumés and conducting employment interviews and background checks are covered, as well as how to make a job offer to the top applicant.

Chapter 2 delves into the many federal employment laws and regulatory agencies that govern almost every step of workplace protocol. From abiding by wage and benefit laws to verifying Social Security numbers and ensuring workplace safety, managers are often saddled with the complex tasks of reporting and compliance to meet these federal requirements. Let's presume that most laws are easier to comply with when managers understand the reasons behind them.

Chapter 2 also begins the discussion of potential workplace legal pitfalls, a discussion that continues in various forms in Chapters 3, 6, 8, and 10. Whenever managers deal with human beings, they deal with the emotions, perceptions, and prejudices of their workers as individuals. It's a wonder a store sells anything at all for all the squabbling and complaining that goes on behind the scenes in some retail workplaces. Recognizing this, we detail numerous problems that fall on managers to prevent, remedy, and/or investigate, including the following list:

- **Chapter 2.** Discrimination, sexual harassment, and wrongful discharge allegations
- **Chapter 3.** Competition among coworkers as a negative force; the tendency of companies to run as hierarchies
- **Chapter 6.** Festering unhappiness in the workplace based on stress, overwork, and lack of flexibility, as well as challenges with new employees who may lack even the most basic skills, such as etiquette and personal responsibility
- **Chapter 8.** The perils of drug abuse (and drug testing), off-the-clock work, and workplace violence; the health-versus-rights debate about smokers on the job; and ways to defuse personality conflicts
- **Chapter 10.** The impact of technology on employees' privacy rights, including cameras, cellular phones, and Internet use on the job, as well as polygraph testing and identity checks

Even in businesses that run smoothly, what the reader will find in this book is proof that written policies about human resource issues (and fair enforcement of them) go a long way toward minimizing problems by minimizing miscommunication, misunderstandings, and rumors.

Other parts of the book cover many of the routine interactions faced by retail managers. For instance, Chapter 4 gives an introduction to labor unions, their representatives, and grievance investigation procedures. Chapter 5 covers every possible type of employee benefit, both financial and lifestyle-related, that companies now offer to their workforces. Today's workers expect flexibility, and retailers have found plenty of ways to give it to them.

Several chapters of the book focus on creative ways to introduce morale-boosting changes to a department or sales force that may be struggling or, at least, not achieving all that its members are capable of. Chapter 7 points out that employees exhibit greater loyalty and passion for companies that embody ethics and sound values. This includes a sense of community spirit and environmental concern, as well as personal commitments to accountability and fiscal responsibility—from the top down.

In Chapter 9, our focus shifts to the customer—what he or she expects from the retail shopping experience (both turn-ons and turn-offs), and how these are impacted directly by store employees' commitments to service. Again, the issue of change is introduced: In workplaces where constancy is valued more than adaptability, things often don't improve when they need to. Of course, this includes service, and the training and motivation it takes to "fire up" the workforce.

The book ends with examples of new trends in retail stores that are turning heads for great customer service in this hugely competitive industry. The chapters leading up to these examples summarize almost every skill it will take for a retail manager to look at the trendiest shops and concepts and proclaim: "My team can do that, too!"

# EMPLOYEE MANAGEMENT

## and Customer Service in the Retail Industry

# HIRING
# GOOD PEOPLE

No matter what is said about the impressive capabilities and business benefits of technology, without good people to manage these assets, most companies would quickly cease to exist. The effectiveness of most departments, teams, and businesses are direct reflections of the character, skills, and motivation of their (very human) staff members. In this chapter, we examine what it takes to locate and hire people who can be trusted to do the specific jobs a retail business requires. This entails the following steps:

- How to write a job description
- Where to find prospective employees

1

- How to analyze résumés
- How to conduct employment interviews
- How to conduct background checks
- How to make a job offer

The late Katharine Graham, longtime owner and publisher of the *Washington Post*, once told an interviewer, "To love what you do and feel that it matters—how could anything be more fun?"[1] But in far too many retail establishments, the average customer can't help but notice the employees don't appear to share Graham's enthusiasm. The shopper wanders around, goods in hand, trying to find someone to answer a question or ring up a sale. When that person is finally located, he or she goes through the motions as if in a daze—or worse, like having been asked to provide service is an extreme hassle.

To a manager, it is clear there are a number of problems that might have contributed to this situation. The day's work schedule could have been made incorrectly. Someone might have called in sick, leaving a department unintentionally short-staffed. The employee who was located might not have been sufficiently trained, or might have been from a different department altogether. He or she might simply be having a bad day.

Just for argument's sake, though, let's say none of these were the case. Let's say the problem is with the person who was hired in the first place. Every business has "problem employees." They are the pessimists who drag everyone else down by being cynical; the deadbeats who seem to do as little actual work as possible; the busybodies who delight in spreading or fueling rumors, and so on. In this chapter, our goal is to keep you from hiring these people!

## THE JOB DESCRIPTION

A floor salesperson is needed to fill an open position. Many store owners or managers assume it is sufficient to advertise in a local newspaper and choose from the parade of folks who happen to see and answer the ad. It quickly becomes apparent that many of them are not qualified.

It would save both managers and job applicants a great deal of time and stress if managers drafted a written job description before a position is advertised that clarifies exactly what is needed before the search begins. Job descriptions are not exactly scintillating reading. Often, they are simply lists of the tasks a person will perform and skills required to perform them correctly. Nonetheless, a job description should be the first step in the hiring process.

After the manager decides on a job title for the position, he or she next composes the job description. The process should begin with a **task analysis**, which lists the worker's responsibilities, along with each task that is performed as part of a particular job—the purpose of the task, how it is done, and what skills and equipment are needed to do it.

The task analysis leads to decisions about the amounts of *education and experience* required for the position. In writing, summarize the knowledge, skills, and abilities the person must have to do the job. A retailer must decide whether to look for a person with "potential" and train him or her, or seek someone who already has worked in the particular field and is familiar with the products and competitors. Some jobs also have physical requirements, such as hand-eye coordination or the ability to lift a certain amount of weight. Some have specialized requirements, such as proficiency with a particular computer program or the flexibility to travel to multiple locations. If travel is required, decide on the percentage of time a person would be expected to be away from home.

The next step is a bit tougher to verbalize than the nuts-and-bolts requirements. The *personal characteristics* of applicants indicate how they will approach the job, what kind of attitude and demeanor the applicant has, and how well they are able to work with other team members. This does not mean how friendly they are; rather, it is a written list of traits and work styles that are desired *for this position*.

One way to accomplish this is to ask for help from the people with whom the new hire would work. They can put together their own individual lists of desired traits, then compare and prioritize them, creating a "master list" for the job description. Personal characteristics involve the person's level of creativity, interpersonal skills, communication style, decision-making style, ability to work under pressure, career goals or motivation level, energy level, and his or her overall attitude, to name a few. Often, a sense of humor is cited as necessary!

Job descriptions are rounded out with basic information about where the person "fits" within the company. In which department does the person work? Who is his or her supervisor? What hours does the person work? Is there an automatic probation period for brand-new workers and, if so, for how long? Pay rates and benefit information are sometimes included in internal job descriptions, but not always when a job is advertised externally.

A couple of caveats: First, avoid writing a job description that fits the person who happens to be leaving and is creating the opening. The hiring process is a great opportunity to discuss what might make the position even more effective in the company and to look for these strengths in the new hire. Second, a thoughtful job description helps managers resist the temptation to hire the applicant who seems to be the most "like them," simply because they have a lot in common—same age range, alma mater, and so on. Sticking to a carefully drafted list of requirements makes it easier to be fair in the hiring process.

Try not to think of writing job descriptions as drudgery. A side benefit of examining each job in detail is that it can provide a valuable overview of the work itself. Is it too much for one person? Not enough to fill an eight-hour workday, but plenty for a part-timer? Do responsibilities overlap where they should not? A good job description will also be useful when you are doing employee reviews.

The job description gives the manager a solid outline for drafting questions to ask during employment interviews. It also allows prospective workers a first glimpse of exactly what they're applying for. As a retail manager, it is your responsibility to ensure that this first glimpse is concise, fair, accurate, and fully professional. Anything less may give would-be employees an unfavorable impression of the company.

## FINDING EMPLOYEES

The good news is, there are many people who want to work in retail. The bad news is, they seem to be scarce when they are needed. The National Restaurant Association has conducted surveys over the years indicating that the retail, foodservice, and health care industries compete for the same groups of employees, which the NRA categorizes thusly:

- *Careerists,* or people who enjoy the industry and want to remain in it.
- *Undecided*, or people who avoid the typical career "issues" by choosing to have a series of jobs rather than a career, per se.
- *Pass-throughs,* or people who have career goals in other occupations but are working in food service or retail temporarily.
- *The misplaced,* or those who are not well suited to the industry but plan to remain in it nonetheless.[2]

Put that way, three of the four categories of workers certainly do not sound like management material! But look closer and you will see that retail has positive aspects that attract these people, and others—students, spouses with children who work staggered shifts so they can share child care, retirees from other jobs who need a second income or are bored with retirement—in addition to the career path managers, retail buyers, and store owners. Which one you are looking for depends on the job description you have created.

The more closely the "help wanted" information is targeted to your ideal candidate, the fewer numbers of applicants you will get—and the better qualified they will be. This includes the wording of the advertisement, but also its placement with these venues, depending on whether the candidate search is local, regional, or national:

- Newspapers
- Your company Web site
- Internet job-search sites
- Trade publications
- Professional associations
- Recruiters and private employment agencies
- Temporary agencies
- The state unemployment office
- College employment and internship programs

Remember, blanketing all of these sites and agencies with the news that your company is hiring only guarantees a glut of résumés to wade through. It is better to select two venues to begin a search. If they don't net the results you need, try the alternates one at a time. Determine their effectiveness based on numbers of incoming responses (and cost) and note that information for filling future job openings.

Most companies use recruiters and private agencies only for senior management positions, since they charge a fee to do the legwork that delivers prescreened, prequalified candidates. However, a few companies feel the cost of so-called headhunters is worth the caliber of candidates they receive, even for entry-level positions. Barry Steinberg, president of Direct Tire & Auto Service, used a headhunting firm when starting his independent chain of stores in Massachusetts, calling it an investment. Steinberg says his goal was to ensure that every person in his operation was so highly qualified that, if they wanted to, they could get a job anywhere. Of course, they don't—Steinberg treats them like business partners instead of employees, so there is very little turnover in his organization. The quality of service is also high enough that Direct

## NEWSPAPER AD—EXPERIENCED SALESPERSON

Foodservice marketing and distribution company seeking an experienced Category Manager to ensure success for customers in achieving strategic sales, marketing and purchasing goals. Candidates MUST have a minimum of 5+ years of successful foodservice distribution or purchasing experience; excellent skills in Microsoft Excel, Word, and Outlook; proven customer service, communication and organizational skills; and be self-motivated with strong initiative and drive. A B.A. degree in marketing or business preferred. Occasional travel required. Background checks and skills testing required for employment. Please email or fax resume and salary history to . . .

Tire & Auto can charge prices 10 to 12 percent higher than its competitors and still thrive.

There are other key sources of employable people that don't require advertising and should not be overlooked:

- Current employees who may be qualified for a change and willing to make it.
- Current employees' personal recommendations of people they know.
- Former employees who left on good terms and whose situation may have changed such that they'd be willing to come back.
- People in other service industries with whom you do business. If they've impressed *you* as their customer, ask if they've ever considered a job change. What could it hurt?

If an advertisement does need to be placed, its length and content depends on the venue. Newspaper ads are typically short because the company pays by the word for them. On the Internet, they can afford to go into greater detail. Some examples (which happen to be gleaned today, as this chapter is being written) are shown in this section of the book.

## Considering Résumés

It is our opinion that the common business practices of computerized sorting of résumés based on certain keywords and rejecting applicants immediately if they don't have college degrees ensure that a business will miss out on some excellent candidates simply because their career paths may have been less traditional—or they haven't read the latest business articles about the "right" keywords to include. However, busy human resources departments often take the easy way out by using these tactics.

## INTERNET JOB POSTING—
## ENTRY-LEVEL, DEPARTMENT STORE

Location: (name of mall and city)

Position type: Full or part-time

Become a part of our most fashion-forward department! This is an entry-level position in a fun, trendy area. Retail experience helpful but not required. Possible advancement to other departments with experience.

Requirements: The ideal candidate for the position must have a positive, energetic personality and desire to be a growing part of this very successful store. The ability to approach customers, build sales, and close the sale is required. We also expect all associates to share in basic merchandising, department operations and presentation standards.

Résumés should be sorted instead for the basics: spelling and grammar, punctuation, neatness and good formatting, the ability to communicate clearly, and a first-pass look at how well the person's credentials actually meet the posted job description. If your company requires a specific job application be submitted, pay attention to whether the candidate followed the instructions, wrote clearly, spelled things correctly, and answered all pertinent questions when filling it out.

Those that make the first cut must then be examined in greater detail. Harvard Graduate School of Business Administration professor Christopher Bartlett suggests looking for

- Signs of achievement and results; for example, a profit orientation, stability, or progressive career momentum
- A career goal in line with the job being offered
- A strong overall construction and clean appearance (this refers to the résumé, not the candidate!)[3]

Bartlett adds that résumés with unexplained employment gaps, multiple short-term jobs, and a career path that doesn't seem particularly logical may signal problems, while lengthy descriptions of education or personal information probably mean the candidate hasn't had much work experience.

Corporate recruiters say the modern, well-crafted résumé may be reworded as needed to fit each job but must always include the following:

## INTERNET JOB POSTING—RETAIL STORE MANAGER

(THIS COMPANY) has excellent career opportunities available for entrepreneurial Retail Store Managers who display a high energy level, self-motivation and the desire to succeed. Enjoy a performance-based sales pay plan with special incentives which reward you for your performance.

### TRAINING

As a Manager In Training, you are focused on developing the skills to become a Store Manager. This includes learning how to Operate The Store, Build Your Team, and Serve The Customers. Our Manager In Training Program is geared toward your individual needs and professional development. You will be provided with interactive training, which will include classroom seminars, broadcasts from the Home Office, presentations by management covering most facets of store operations, and manager training meetings held by the District Manager.

### REQUIREMENTS

Entry-level **Managers In Training** will have the potential to qualify for store management in as little as 6 to 9 months. These positions require:

- One year management or related work experience or one year college

- Excellent interpersonal and communication skills

- Must be reliable and have high personal integrity

- Must be computer-literate

- High school diploma or equivalent

- A proven track record in commission-based retail sales is highly desired

- Must have demonstrated leadership characteristics, including aptitude to lead a sales team, multi-task, and manage sales and the business

- Must be 18 years of age or older

Additional positions may be available in selected markets for **Experienced Manager In Training** candidates, with potential to promote to Store Manager in 3-6 months. To qualify for these fast-track opportunities, you must meet the requirements listed above, plus have at least one of these:

- Minimum of 3 years retail store management experience

- 4 year college degree

- Minimum of 10 years military experience

Continued

Ability to work a flexible retail schedule, including some evenings, weekends and/or holidays, is needed for all positions. Application process includes background check, consisting of criminal and credit history and reference checks. Drug testing is also required in some areas.

We offer excellent benefits, including medical, dental, life, and vision insurance, paid vacation and holidays, 401(K) plan, tuition reimbursement program, employee discount, credit union, plus more. We are an equal opportunity employer dedicated to diversity in the workplace.

- A career summary or introductory statement, making it clear what type of position the person is seeking and why he or she is qualified for the job.
- Keywords a computerized screening system is likely to recognize. These are typically the "most important" nouns and technical phrases in the written job description.
- Specific examples of successes and results, not just a list of employers, job titles, and employment dates.
- An objective, uncluttered writing style that eliminates all personal pronouns and articles—"I," "my," "the," "a," and so on. The theory here is that the resulting copy is tighter and less personal, focusing on what a person excels at instead of who they are.
- Work history in reverse chronological order, emphasizing achievements.[4]

Most people include references on their resumés, but "early on" is not the time for checking them. It's best to interview the person first, then confirm what was said in the interview by calling the references.

As with creation of a job description, it is best to have several people look at the same stack of résumés and make their choices and notes, then discuss them as a group before proceeding to the all-important interview phase of the hiring process. A polite letter should be sent promptly to applicants who have been rejected. Many companies today skip this all-important step, but it is not advisable. Even if it is a form letter, it should be signed by a human.

Have you ever been unemployed? Then you probably realize how important it is to track the results of your search, and even learn from them. Many job searchers are not comfortable papering the market with résumés—they send one or two at a time and expect a company to announce its intentions before they "feel right" about applying elsewhere.

If their initial application is not even acknowledged, what kind of public relations impact does that have? In retail, you've probably not only lost a prospective employee but a customer as well.

An additional important note is to be well organized about the way in which résumés and job applications are kept on file as they are received. The U.S. Civil Rights Act requires applications be retained for at least six months after a job is filled, even those of the applicants who were not hired. The Age Discrimination Act requires that applications be kept for a full year. You will learn more about these and other federal employment laws in Chapter 2.

## INTERVIEWING JOB CANDIDATES

Some companies prefer to do short initial interviews by telephone. This first step is another screening tool that helps determine the candidate's suitability for the job and his or her ability to communicate, but it is never preferable to an in-person interview.

Résumé information should be used to script out some specific questions for each applicant in addition to those asked of all job candidates. When you interview candidates, you are looking at several, equally critical aspects of their employment potential:

- Their skills and work experiences
- Their interest in your company and this position in particular
- Their attitude, energy, motivation, and goals
- Their personal appearance and demeanor (specifically, its appropriateness for the job for which they are applying)

There are three types of job interviews: structured, unstructured, and a combination of both. In a structured interview, every candidate is asked the same list of questions so their answers may be compared exactly. An unstructured interview works more like a conversation, with each candidate's responses prompting follow-up questions that lead in whatever direction the conversation goes. It's probably more interesting for the interviewer, but there is a risk that some topics won't be covered. That is why most companies choose a combination format.

Plan to spend from 30 to 60 minutes on an interview. There is no need to hit prospective new hires with the infamous Donald Trump question—"How brilliant are you?"—but keep the focus on the people, the attributes they believe make them right for this job, and what the candidate expects from an employer. Remember to use the two written documents you have—the job description itself and the person's résumé or application—as the basis for discussion.

The feeling you want as an interviewer is an overall sense of professionalism from the person. Look for clues about whether the candidate's work habits will translate well to your business environment. Ask questions about the candidate's sense of ethics and integrity, and ability to learn, change, adapt, and get along with coworkers. Size up the person's level of honesty. Later, you'll have the chance to confirm it with a background check.

## WHAT *NOT* TO ASK

There are plenty of topics to discuss in a job interview, and also plenty that are either inappropriate or downright illegal according to myriad federal employment laws. While it is tempting and even natural to want to chat with a job candidate about his or her children, marital status, or the fact that you saw the person at a political rally or church service recently, it is smarter to avoid any of the topics on the following list—even if the candidate brings it up or mentions it on his or her résumé:

| | |
|---|---|
| Age | Religious affiliations |
| Marital status | Child care arrangements |
| Race, ethnicity, ancestry | Arrests or convictions |
| Children or intention to | Citizenship |
|   have them | Medical conditions |
| Physical or mental disabilities | Church or club memberships |
| Use of alcohol or tobacco | Whether wages are being garnished |
| Education | Political affiliations |

In short, keep the questions focused on information that is directly related to the job. Some of these topics (such as age and physical limitations) can be covered after a person is hired—but never before.

Take notes as the interview progresses, but not at the expense of eye contact and being a good listener.

Another necessary component of the interview is to give the job seeker a chance to ask questions about the company and the open position. Their interest level should be evident, and the caliber of their questions should be noted. The interview may even include a short tour of the facility. If specific skills tests are administered, this is the time to do them.

## Checking References

The in-person interview reduces the applicant pool even further. The references of the remaining candidates should be contacted at this point. The main reason for this is to verify the accuracy of the information provided by the applicant. Remember, however, that most human resources and supervisory personnel have been advised by their legal departments to say very little about former employees. The most you will probably get is a confirmation of employment dates and salary. Still, it can't hurt to ask for confirmation of something the candidate mentioned in an interview: "Betsy said she was part of a layoff that involved 100 workers. Can you confirm that?"

Federal law does require a former employer to accurately respond to questions about drug tests—whether the person took one, refused one, or tested positive for drug use—if the job requires driving a vehicle with a commercial license, such as a truck driver for a retailer's warehouse facility. [5]

One interesting way to get around all this legal tiptoeing comes from the book *Hiring Smart!* by Pierre Mornell.[6] Mornell suggests that a manager leave a message for the reference at a time he or she is unlikely to get a human on the telephone—say, at lunchtime. Mention the name of the applicant and the particular position. Conclude the message by saying, "Your name has been given as a reference. Please call me back if the candidate was outstanding."

Ingenious! Generally, Mornell says, people will call back promptly because they want to be helpful to a job seeker who was an excellent employee. If not, their silence is telling—without saying a word or testing their companies' legal liability by saying the "wrong" thing.

## The Follow-up Interview

The few candidates who make the final cut return for follow-up interviews that should focus less on specific experience and more on behavioral topics—that is, how candidates handle stress, success, and failure; what their work ethic is; how they problem-solve; and what kind of team member they might be. Jacobi Kelley Personnel in Tulsa, Oklahoma, suggests questions like these:

- Describe a time on any job in which you were faced with problems or stresses that tested your coping skills.
- Give me an example of an important goal you set in the past and tell me about your success in reaching it.[7]

In short, draft self-appraisal questions for this interview that prompt the applicant to interpret and adapt the facts about his or her skills and experience to *this* job and *this* workplace. Again, resist the temptation to be impressed by credentials and/or how much the person seems to have in common with you. Think instead about how well he or she *uses* those credentials in real-world employment situations. Does this person fit your vision for what the department or team needs and where the company is headed overall? Why do they feel they are the best person to help the company meet its goals? Well, why not ask the candidate? After all, that is the point of the second (and usually final) interview.

Behavioral interviews are often done by teams of two or three instead of a single manager. The more input, the better. Some companies choose to do team interviewing as a legal precaution as well.

## BACKGROUND CHECKS

Another legal precaution that has become more commonplace in today's working world is the background check of prospective employees. *Negligent hiring* lawsuits are on the rise—that is, if a person is hired and his or her actions end up hurting others through injury, a crime, sexual harassment, and so on. Corporate financial scandals, child abductions, terrorist acts, and identity thefts have all made employers more willing to look into the criminal, financial, and legal background of prospective workers as well as whatever is on their résumés. In some cases, federal and/or state law *requires* a background check—for jobs that entail working with children, the elderly, or disabled persons. While this does not often apply in retail, there are plenty of good reasons to check someone out thoroughly before making a job offer.

There are many companies that specialize in background checks, and a lot of retailers hire them rather than doing their own investigations. These third-party companies are subject to the federal **Fair Credit Reporting Act** (FCRA), but as with any type of business, there are good ones and bad ones. They range from individual "private investigators" to huge, online data brokers. Their thoroughness, and the accuracy of the information received, should be your primary concerns as an employer.

Before a third-party background check is performed, the employer must get the written authorization of the applicant. Most companies ask for this signature as part of their standard job application process—although the consent form that requests the background check must be on a *separate page*, not part of the job application itself.

A third-party report (called a "consumer report" in the FCRA law) usually involves a criminal record check. It can also include the person's credit report and usually confirms his or her Social Security number, most recent addresses, and so on. The credit report may include civil lawsuits and judgments, tax liens, and accounts that have been placed for collection for the past seven years, but (by law) no farther back than that.

Under federal law, convictions are not dropped from a person's record, no matter how old the conviction, but third-party screening companies are not allowed to report arrest records for more than seven years. State laws may vary. There are other types of records that you might be able to access, but only if you receive written permission from the candidate to check them, namely education records (except for directory records), medical records, and military service records (except for basic details). Any retailer should consult an attorney about how to ask questions related to legal problems, as well as how an applicant's answers should be weighed. Some applicants find out the hard way that a DUI (driving under the influence) or DWI (driving while intoxicated) conviction follows them and is not considered a minor traffic violation, even if it happened decades earlier.

A prospective employer risks a lawsuit if they use any of the following to reject an otherwise qualified candidate for a job:

- Workers' compensation claims—the fact that the person filed them or was ever paid workers' compensation
- Medical information
- Bankruptcy filings

If something in a background check is troublesome enough to reject a job candidate, it is best to let the person know about it. In fact, if he or she signed the form allowing the check in the first place, the candidate is entitled to a copy of the consumer report. There have been cases in which people looking for work go unemployed because there is incorrect information on their background report—from identity theft, for example—and no one bothers to tell them.[8] The Federal Trade Commission has specific guidelines for disclosure of information, and enforces the FCRA.[9]

## SELECTING A CANDIDATE

Rarely do job interviews or background checks drag into the months, with three or four callbacks for the last few promising applicants—although it does happen. Most often, there is not enough time to drag one's corporate feet. This does not mean that the first fairly well qualified warm body with a decent credit report should get the job.

By the end of a second interview, if the race is too close to call (so to speak), it is time to decide . . . exactly why you haven't decided yet! Pinpoint the information you lack, and decide how to go about getting it promptly. This may involve scripting out several more tough questions to ask of each finalist in a third interview, perhaps with a team doing the questioning.

When a consensus is reached, it is time to make the job offer. Usually this begins with a congratulatory phone call, but it should be followed up with a written offer letter. Many companies have their own offer letter formats, although this is not necessary. The letter should include

- A reiteration of the job title and responsibilities
- Start date and work hours, if applicable
- Compensation and/or pay rate (per hour, per month, etc.)
- A brief explanation of employee benefits offered by the company
- A line or two about whether an employment contract will need to be signed
- A deadline to respond to the offer
- Instructions for how to respond to the offer (in writing, by calling a certain person, etc.)
- Necessary next steps (if required)—an employee orientation, a drug test, and so forth.

The candidates who were not selected should receive either a phone call or a letter—and these should be at least slightly personalized, not form letters. If they were called back for a second or third interview, they made it far enough through the hiring process to be personally informed that they were not chosen. You are not required to go into the particulars, but they may ask, so be prepared with a courteous (if nonspecific) answer. Thank them sincerely for their time and interest in the company. Be sure to mention that you will keep their résumé on file and contact them if a similar position opens in the near future. This is not only good public relations; it is a smart way to maintain a pool of prequalified applicants.

## CHAPTER SUMMARY

A "good" employee improves a company by having the skills and attitude that are a good fit for their job. This is why a thorough and accurate job description must be written for every position before it is advertised.

Managers looking for workers will be unable to identify a "good fit" when it walks through the door if they can't match the optimum skills to the required tasks.

This chapter explained the multiple uses of job descriptions—to give retail managers an overview of their workforce, as a starting point for job interviews, and as a backup for the employee review process. The chapter included sample advertisements and job requirement lists, and mentioned where to place employment ads as well as options for seeking job candidates without advertising or hiring recruiters.

A two-part process for reviewing was outlined, including a first look at grammar, spelling, and matching qualifications to the job description, followed by an in-depth look at education and work experience. Possible red flags and proper formatting techniques were also discussed.

Techniques for successful interviews and reference checks were covered, including specifics about the types of background information employers seek about applicants and what can (and cannot) be used to evaluate them. The chapter ended with a rundown of what a job offer letter should contain when the "right person" is finally selected.

## DISCUSSION QUESTIONS

1. Write a job description for the last job (either paying or volunteer) that you have had.
2. Why does the ad for a retail store manager specify an "entrepreneurial" person is necessary, when this is clearly not an opportunity for self-employment?
3. If a prospective employer began an interview by asking, "How brilliant are you?" what would *you* say?
4. As a store manager, would you choose to do job interviews alone or with others? How many others? Explain your reasoning.
5. As a job seeker, what questions would you ask of a prospective employer? List 10 of them—and make them tough! Now look at the questions as an interviewer (or hand them to a classmate to play the "interviewer" role) and write a line or two about what each question says about the applicant.

# ENDNOTES

1. *The New York Public Library Book of 20th Century American Quotations* (New York: The Stonesong Press, Inc. and the New York Public Library, 1992).
2. The National Restaurant Association, Chicago, Illinois, 1997.
3. Christopher Bartlett, *Harvard Business Essentials Manager's Toolkit* (Boston: Harvard Business School Publishing Corporation, Boston, Massachusetts, 2004).
4. Kate Lorenz, *Seven Signs It's Time to Toss Your Resumé*, MSN Careers, CareerBuilder.com, 2005.
5. *Fact Sheet 16: Employment Background Checks*, Privacy Rights Clearinghouse, San Diego, California, June 2004, http://www.privacyrights.org/fs/fs16–bck.htm.
6. Pierre Mornell, *Hiring Smart!* (Berkeley, CA: Ten Speed Press, 1998).
7. Jacobi Kelley Personnel, *Behavioral Interview Sample*, Tulsa, Oklahoma, ©1997–2005).
8. See endnote 5.
9. Federal Trade Commission. *Using Consumer Reports: What Employers Need to Know* (1999), www.ftc.gov/bcp/online/pubs/buspubs/credempl.htm.

# 2

# FEDERAL EMPLOYMENT LAWS

One of the biggest challenges facing retail managers is keeping track of and complying with the myriad labor laws and regulations that govern various businesses and industries. There are literally hundreds of these laws, and most of them have differing sets of compliance and reporting rules. In this chapter, you learn about the major federal laws that involve employees, including:

- Wage and benefit-related laws
- Health- and safety-related laws

■ Antidiscrimination laws
■ Sexual harassment and wrongful discharge policies

This chapter includes information about a manager's role in compliance with these laws, as well as some of the controversies about the laws. Of course, it is beyond the scope of this textbook to examine the labor laws of all 50 states, or even comprehensively address the 180+ federal laws that relate to labor—although details about many of the federal laws can be found on the Department of Labor (DOL) Web site (www.dol.gov). Here's a partial list of them, just to illustrate how much time and effort managers must devote to gaining even a basic understanding of their compliance and reporting responsibilities:

Consumer Credit Protection Act
Contract Work Hours and Safety Standards Act
Copeland "Anti-Kickback" Act
Davis-Bacon and Related Acts (DBRA)
Employee Polygraph Protection Act (EPPA)
Employee Retirement Income Security Act (ERISA)
Energy Employees Occupational Illness Compensation Program
Fair Credit Reporting Act (FCRA, mentioned in Chapter 1)
Fair Labor Standards Act (FLSA)
Fair Labor Standards Act (FLSA)/Child Labor
Family and Medical Leave Act (FMLA)
Federal Employees' Compensation Act (FECA)
Federal Mine Safety and Health Act
Immigration and Nationality Act
Labor-Management Reporting and Disclosure Act (LMRDA)
Longshore and Harbor Workers' Compensation Act (LHWCA)
McNamara-O'Hara Service Contract Act (SCA)
Migrant and Seasonal Agricultural Worker Protection Act (MSPA)
Occupational Safety and Health Act (OSH, not to be confused with OSHA, the
    agency that administers it)
Rehabilitation Act of 1973, Section 503
Uniformed Services Employment and Reemployment Rights Act (USERRA)
Vietnam Era Veterans' Readjustment Assistance Act (VEVRAA)
Walsh-Healey Public Contracts Act
Worker Adjustment and Retraining Notification Act (WARN)

It's obvious from their names that not all of these apply to retail situations. But the point is, there are rules aplenty! What follows is a summary of the major laws and regulations that address workplace issues and activities for more than 125 million American workers of all kinds. It is intended to give managers an overview of the most commonly used federal labor laws and regulations, not to provide comprehensive descriptions and/or interpretations. It is incumbent upon managers, no matter what their level in the retail industry, to determine which of the laws are relevant to them, and then educate themselves to the point that they can competently comply with them.

## FEDERAL WAGE-RELATED LAWS

The **Fair Labor Standards Act** (FLSA) became law in 1938 to set standards and regulate minimum wages, overtime pay, and child labor for most businesses—those with at least two employees that produce goods for interstate commerce. The FLSA requires employers to pay at least the federal minimum hourly wage (which has been $5.15 since September 1997) and overtime pay of one and one-half times the regular rate of pay.

The FLSA limits the hours children under age 16 can work in nonagricultural jobs, and also limits children under age 18 from working in dangerous jobs. The FLSA is administered by the DOL Employment Standards Administration's Wage and Hour Division. This division also enforces labor standards provisions in the Immigration and Nationality Act that apply to nonimmigrant visa programs, most commonly known by their abbreviations: H-1B, H-1C, and H-2A.

The *minimum wage* is a base pay rate set by Congress that can become complicated for employers because it does not apply to administrators, professionals, executives, outside sales representatives, or food service employees who work for tips. There is also a provision to pay a 180-day subminimum "training wage" to employees 19 and younger, although employers seldom use it. The other complicating factor surrounding the federal minimum wage is that it does not supersede state minimum wage laws that set a higher hourly rate than the federal law.

*Overtime pay* is set by the federal government at one and one-half times an employee's regular pay for hours worked beyond 40 per week, to include certain "portal to portal" before-and-after work tasks if those tasks are standard in a given industry or included in an employment agreement.

Fair pay for time worked has become a big employment issue. In the past decade, there have been record settlements in wage-and-hour lawsuits and judgments. The disagreements that have arisen to become class action lawsuits have included

- Inaccurately calculating employees' "regular" rate of pay.
- Misclassifying employees as independent contractors or otherwise "exempt."
- Not providing lunch breaks. (Federal law requires a one-half hour meal break during a full-time workday, or the employee must be paid for the time.)
- Annual bonuses paid to salaried workers and their impact on how calculation of overtime pay.
- Exempting managers from overtime pay and other provisions because they are salaried.[1]

The turn of the current century brought settlements of $20 million paid by RiteAid stores, $90 million for Farmer's Insurance, and $3 million for Rent-A-Center stores, all resulting from various wage and hour lawsuits.

*Child Labor Regulations* in the FLSA are specifically designed to protect children from working long hours, in hazardous occupations, or during time frames that would prevent them from attending school. There are exceptions and special rules for farm children, actors, entertainers, newspaper carriers, and children working for their parents.

Where retailers are often unclear is in summer or after-school hiring situations with underage employees—for example, the friend's teenager who wants work experience and is a bright kid who deserves consideration. Generally, the following rules apply:

- Minors 14 to 16 years old can work limited hours in nonhazardous, nonmanufacturing, or nonmining jobs.
- Minors 16 to18 years old can work any hours in nonhazardous jobs.

The federal government enforces the FLSA through the DOL, which can impose injunctive relief and restitution of back pay for injured employees. Employees may also sue on their own behalf to recover back wages, overtime, liquidated damages, reinstatement, and legal fees. DOL also imposes fines for violations, particularly in the area of child labor.

## Other Wage-related Acts and Regulations

Several statutes have been enacted for employees not covered by the FLSA, although they don't often apply in retail situations. Most federal contracts, for example, include provisions requiring FLSA minimum wages. The **Walsh-Healy Act** requires manufacturers and sellers (which may include retailers) to use the wage guidelines if they supply the federal government with goods or services valued at $10,000 or more. The **Davis-Bacon Act** also requires a minimum wage, usually based on local union construction worker wages, for companies with federal building contracts larger than $2,000.

## FEDERAL HEALTH AND SAFETY LAWS

The **Occupational Safety and Health Act** (OSH) was passed in 1970 to make employers responsible for providing workplaces that are free from recognized, serious hazards. The OSH regulates workplace safety and health conditions for most private industries, and has provisions for OSHA-approved state systems to cover public-sector workers.

The Occupational Safety and Health Administration (OSHA) oversees and enforces compliance with OSH regulations, and safety and health standards. An OSHA inspection is usually triggered by employee complaints or in the event of a workplace death or serious injury. Most visits are unannounced, and warrants can be issued if an employer refuses access to OSHA inspectors. If violations are found, employers can be criminally prosecuted, fined, or given deadlines by which to correct them. Employers can answer a deadline with a written "notice of contest" within 15 days of their citation. The case then goes to a hearing, and depending on the outcome, employers can appeal the findings all the way up to the U.S. Court of Appeals.

Retail businesses have not been a big priority for OSHA. In 2003, John L. Henshaw of OSHA told members of the International Mass Retail Association that OSHA had conducted 660 inspections of retail stores in the previous year, about 2 percent of the total number of inspections. He said the issues of greatest concern were exits, housekeeping problems, and electrical hazards.

Henshaw also discussed the agency's formation of a number of industry partnerships to work specifically on ergonomics, since musculoskeletal injuries account for about one-third of injuries in the U.S. workforce every year. Retail supermarkets were among the first groups targeted for prevention efforts.[2]

Most federal labor laws include protections for whistle-blowers—that is, employees who report violations of law by their employers—and OSHA is usually the agency that enforces whistle-blower protections.

## The Family and Medical Leave Act

When an injury or other medical problem occurs, or when a new baby arrives, the **Family and Medical Leave Act** requires companies with more than 50 employees to provide up to 12 weeks of unpaid but job-protected leave for eligible employees. The circumstances can be the adoption or birth of a child, or a serious illness of the employee or a spouse, child, or parent. The FMLA also requires the companies to maintain health care benefits during the leave period, if those benefits were part of the employee's basic compensation package.

Employees must give 30 days' notice of the impending leave if their upcoming absence is foreseeable. Exemptions to these requirements include employees who have worked less than 24 hours a week during the preceding year, or who have worked for the company less than one year; schoolteachers or other instructors during the school year; employees whose salaries or wages fall within the top 10 percent of the company's employees; or employees whose spouses work at the same company. In the latter case, they can take a total of 12 weeks between them.

The act requires that employees returning from leave must be given the same or a similar position, not simply the same pay and benefits. Changing job titles, reducing supervisory responsibilities, or increasing clerical work constitutes a different job and does not meet the provisions of the law.

# FEDERAL BENEFITS LAWS

Do you know whether your company's benefit plans are financially secure? The **Employee Retirement Income Security Act** (ERISA) was passed in 1974 to govern private employers who provide pension, health, vacation, and death benefits to workers. Title I of ERISA is administered by DOL's Employee Benefits Security Administration (EBSA) and includes compliance and reporting requirements for the trustees of pension and welfare benefit plans. Unlike the minimum-wage laws, these preempt similar state laws.

ERISA requires certain employers and plan administrators to pay premiums to the federal Pension Benefit Guaranty Corporation (PBGC) to fund insurance systems to protect various types of retirement benefits. EBSA also administers the **Comprehensive Omnibus Budget Reconciliation Act** of 1985. Most people know it as simply "COBRA," the law that allows some former employees, their spouses (and former spouses), dependent children, and retirees to keep their health insurance at group rates, at least temporarily, after a job ends under certain circumstances.

ERISA violations that make headlines usually involve a company's executives mismanaging its pension funds or other benefit plans. The agency has a toll-free hotline employees can call to request assistance or report problems with these plans. In 2003, EBSA handled more than 173,000 inquiries and recovered nearly $83 million in benefits with informal resolution on a case-by-case basis, but the hotline also serves as a source of leads for more serious investigations. EBSA can take administrative corrective actions, or file civil or criminal cases to recover damages—and it does. In 2003, the most recent year for which statistics are available, EBSA closed 175 criminal investigations and 4,253 civil investigations, which netted 137 criminal indictments and $1.4 billion in corrections and recovered benefits. Another 240 companies participated in the Voluntary Fiduciary Correction Program (VFCP), agreeing to self-correct ERISA violations without an enforcement action. That's more than triple the number of companies in the program the previous year.[3]

## The Social Security Act

Perhaps the most hotly debated issue of the 2000s—at least thus far—the **Social Security Act** was passed in 1935 to provide unemployment insurance, and income for retired workers. Social Security retirement benefits initially supplemented pensions and other retirement income, but were not intended to replace all lost income. The Social Security Act has since been amended many times to expand benefits monetarily and to make more people eligible for more reasons.

Eligible persons must apply to the Social Security Administration (SSA) to receive benefits, which can start as early as age 62 for workers (in reduced form), but usually start at 67 to receive the full benefit amount. Children under 18 (or under 19 if the child is still a full-time high school student) can also be awarded benefits based on a deceased parent's contribution to the fund. Benefits may also be paid to severely disabled, unmarried children, spouses over age 62, spouses caring for disabled children or children under 16, and some divorced spouses.

Families are benefit-eligible only if the worker has earned at least six "credits" and worked for at least 10 years. Currently, one credit of coverage is received for each $500 of annual earnings, up to a maximum of four credits earned each year. Having enough credit units to be fully insured, however, does not guarantee that a person will receive the maximum amount of dollar benefits under the program.

All this may change as Congress wrestles with Social Security projections and revamps the entire program for future retirees, but for the time being, benefits a worker or their family receives are based on actual earnings over the worker's career, adjusted to reflect changes in average wages since 1951. If a person keeps working after benefits begin, some or all benefits may be lost if they exceed the earnings limit set by the SSA.

Social Security benefits are paid through employer and employee payroll taxes based on the 1954 **Federal Insurance Contributions Act** (FICA), which requires employers to match the tax withheld from employee paychecks. In fact, employers are responsible for the full amount if they don't withhold sufficient FICA funds from employee paychecks. Violations can mean financial penalties and criminal charges.

When an employer hears from the Social Security Administration, it is often in the form of a so-called **mismatch letter**. This is a letter advising the employer that they have reported a particular Social Security number that doesn't match what the SSA has on file for that worker. It's usually a clerical error, or an employee's failure to properly report a name change to SSA after marriage or divorce; but it may also indicate an identity theft, or some type of fraud involving an undocumented worker. For this reason, employers should periodically compare their employment records to the W-2 forms submitted to the SSA. If they don't match up, they can be corrected on a form called a W-2c. In the rare instance that an employee would admit to document fraud, if you continue to allow them to work for you, you are participating in the fraud.[4]

## Other Social Security–Related Laws

*Medicare* is the popular name given to the SSA's **Title 18: Health Insurance for the Aged and Disabled**, passed by Congress in 1965. It is funded with a combination of Social Security taxes, monthly premiums paid by eligible individuals, and general revenues of the federal government. The program is administered by the Health Care Financing Administration.

All persons over age 65 are eligible for Medicare, along with qualified retirees and disabled persons. Part A of Title 18 covers hospitalization, and services provided by nursing homes, home health care, and hospices. Part B partially pays for outpatient hospital care, doctors' fees, "durable" medical equipment, and other medical supplies and services.

*Medicaid* is the popular name given to the SSA's **Title 19: Grants to the States for Medical Assistance**, also passed by Congress in 1965. Medicaid supplies federal funding to the states for providing aid to low-income persons for medical expenses—but only as long as the state programs follow federal guidelines. Medicaid is not as comprehensive as Medicare, but it does at least partially cover hospital, laboratory, doctor, and nursing costs.

*Unemployment compensation* is the popular name for SSA's **Title 3: Grants to the States for Unemployment Compensation Administration** and **Title 9: Miscellaneous Provisions Relating to Employment Security**. Both were passed by Congress in 1935. States were not required to join the program, but tax credits were given to employers who paid into state unemployment funds—if the states joined the program and followed federal guidelines. Naturally, the states signed up.

Individual states' programs vary, but all are federally approved, and all are similar in that every private-sector employee must be eligible if he or she reaches a certain earnings threshold (not counting exceptions for domestic workers and some farmworkers); and the maximum benefit period cannot exceed 26 weeks.

The **Supplemental Security Income** (SSI) program was passed by Congress in 1974. SSI supplements SSA's primary old-age protection, disability insurance, and survivors insurance, and applies primarily to the blind and disabled, and those who didn't earn enough during their working lives to be eligible for regular Social Security benefits.

## FEDERAL ANTIDISCRIMINATION LAWS

There are numerous federal laws designed to prevent workplace discrimination by employers. Some of the most important include the following.

The **Equal Pay Act of 1963** prohibits employers from paying persons of one sex less than persons of another sex for equal work. It does provide for exceptions based on other criteria, such as seniority, merit, individual sales or production, and other factors not based on sex. An example of the latter exceptions was the 1973 court case *Hodgsen v. Robert Hall Clothes, Inc.*, in which the Third Circuit Court of Appeals held that higher salaries could be paid to male salespeople because of the higher profit margin on men's clothing.

In addition to the exceptions, pay equity or the concept of "comparable worth" are not considered to be valid grounds for a wage discrimination complaint under the act. Comparable worth is the suggestion that jobs traditionally held by one gender are comparable to different jobs traditionally held by the other gender, and thus should be paid at the same rate. This theory may only be used successfully in a class action suit under the current law, not to remedy an individual worker's complaint.

The **Civil Rights Act of 1964** bars employment discrimination based on race, religion, national origin, or gender. It applies to almost all private- and public-sector employees. Only companies or organizations with 15 employees or members are covered by the Civil Rights Act, except for union hiring halls or employment agencies, which can have a single employee and still be covered by the act.

The same legislation established the *Equal Employment Opportunity Commission* (EEOC) to investigate civil rights complaints, attempt to resolve them without legal action, and to enforce the provisions of the act if a settlement cannot be reached. This includes filing discrimination lawsuits in the federal courts. The EEOC also litigates class actions for large groups of employees or established patterns of discrimination, or can issue a "right-to-sue" letter that authorizes a complainant to take private legal action without further EEOC involvement.

The EEOC reported incoming complaints in 2004 as follows:[5]

- Race-based complaints: 27,696
- Gender-based complaints: 24,249
- Religion-based complaints: 2,466
- National origin-based complaints: 8,361

The **Age Discrimination in Employment Act of 1967** bars employers in the public and private sector from age-based discrimination against workers between ages 40 and 70. Exceptions are made when there is a legitimate age-related job qualification, or where a reasonable factor other than age has led to an older worker being passed over for promotion, fired, or not hired. Federal employees older than 70 are covered by this act, too, although private-sector companies and other organizations can still set a mandatory retirement age of 70.

Age discrimination is a growing field in the legal profession because of the growing number of older Americans in the workplace, but they are tough cases to prove. Just because an employer replaces an older worker with a younger one does not automatically mean "age discrimination" has taken place. The older worker must prove that the action was intentional, and specifically because of age.[6] In 2004, the EEOC received 17,837 complaints—but in about 60 percent of the cases, the commission decided there was "no reasonable cause" to pursue the complaint. Others are settled when the older worker agrees to a payment of back pay and/or benefits without filing a suit. Still, in 2004 the EEOC collected $69 million on behalf of age discrimination complainants.

Another age-related federal law is the **Older Workers Benefit Protection Act**, which makes it illegal for employers to force workers to take early retirement, or to reduce their benefits (like health or life insurance) or stop contributing to their pension plans if they choose to work past retirement age. For a company, the only way to make early retirement legal (as well as attractive) to employees over age 40 nowadays is to give them a choice of either staying on the job or retiring with a plan that offers them an even better financial situation than if they continued to work—and then allow employees to make the choice freely. If either choice could be construed as "worse" for the employee, then the offer is not considered legal under the act.

The **Vocational Rehabilitation Act of 1973** requires companies with federal contracts larger than $2,500 to make "good faith" efforts to hire handicapped individuals, and bars discrimination against workers solely by reason of their handicap in any federally funded activity or program.

The act defines handicapped persons as those who

- Have a physical or mental impairment that substantially limits one or more of their major life activities
- Have a record of such impairment
- Are regarded as having such impairment

The act defines discrimination as applying to impairments that don't interfere with the requirements of a given job. Employers are expected to make "reasonable efforts" to accommodate disabled workers (see the upcoming text on the Americans with Disabilities Act for more information), but employees who allege this type of discrimination have the responsibility to prove they can perform all of their job's duties.

The **Pregnancy Discrimination Act of 1978** makes it a federal law that pregnant women must be afforded the same treatment as persons with disabilities. It prohibits employers from discharging or refusing to hire or promote a woman solely because she is pregnant. Pregnant women may voluntarily take time off under the Family and Medical Leave Act or similar state laws, but mandatory leave is allowed only when the woman cannot keep working.

Pregnancy discrimination claims do not outnumber sex discrimination or sexual harassment charges filed with the EEOC, but they do outpace them in overall growth. A number of factors contribute to this trend, including women having children later in life and choosing to remain on the job during their pregnancies, and their disagreements with employers who see pregnancy as a liability or productivity problem. No matter how an employer views the condition of pregnancy, federal law says a manager cannot ask job applicants if they are pregnant and pregnant women don't have to inform their employers of their condition.[7]

When the **Americans with Disabilities Act of 1990** (ADA) was passed by Congress, it effectively expanded the Vocational Rehabilitation Act of 1973 to include all private- and public-sector employers with more than 15 workers, regardless of whether they have federal contracts. The ADA forbids companies from discriminating against job applicants with disabilities that substantially limit their physical or mental capacity, as long as they can actually perform the job for which they apply. It also requires employers to make a "reasonable effort" to accommodate the disabilities of handicapped workers.

The term "disability" has been broadly defined to include obesity, asthma, and a variety of injuries and conditions, and the law still generates confusion in the workplace about its scope and the exact definitions of some of its provisions. There are three practical rules about which retailers should be aware primarily for customers of public facilities—but also for employees:

1. All public accommodation new construction that began after 1992 must meet the ADA's rules for accessibility.
2. Owners and lessees of existing buildings are required to remove architectural barriers to the disabled when it is "readily achievable" to do so.
3. Where this is not "readily achievable," the ADA expressly requires a public accommodation to make its goods, services, facilities, privileges, advantages, and accommodations available through alternative methods where such methods are, again, "readily achievable."

The trouble, of course, stems from what is "readily achievable" and who pays for it in the cases of retail space that is being leased from a building owner. Retailers have been sued for lack of proper signage for disabled persons and for lack of access to stores, restrooms, parking lots, and garages.[8]

The ADA was first enforced in 1992. It began with just over 15,000 complaints per year, which is about the same as are received today by the EEOC. (The most active year was 1995, with almost 20,000 complaints.) As with age discrimination complaints, about 60 percent of ADA complaints are found to have "no reasonable cause" to pursue in court. However, the ADA cases that are either tried or resolved without court action netted $47.7 million in fiscal year 2004.

*Acquired immune deficiency syndrome* (AIDS) is the latest ADA-related challenge. AIDS has been a cause of great concern for employers who provide group health coverage to employees, and over the last 20 years many have tried to reduce their liability by refusing to hire workers with AIDS, or those who test positively for the human immunodeficiency virus (HIV). However, several federal and state laws, including the Americans with Disabilities Act, bar discrimination against workers with AIDS or HIV. Under the ADA, companies cannot test for AIDS/HIV in preemployment screening except in specified circumstances, and as with any other disability, they must reasonably accommodate infected employees so they can keep working.

The **Civil Rights Act of 1991** was passed by Congress in response to a controversial U.S. Supreme Court ruling in 1989. The court decision virtually reversed 20 years' worth of affirmative action rulings that had made it easier for plaintiffs to win employment-related discrimination cases. The principal goal of the act was to reaffirm that racial discrimination and harassment are prohibited in the United States, and that disabled persons and women are eligible for the same compensation and punitive damages that are available to racial minorities, up to a limit of $300,000 for larger companies.

Perhaps ironically, the act does permit companies to discriminate if they can prove reasons that are "job-related" or a "business necessity," so the debate about the scope and definitions of these terms has raged since the act was passed.

This is also the law that bars different thresholds for different groups in test scores and cutoff scores, and forbids test score adjustment on employment-related tests; and it includes the rights of workers to challenge seniority systems they feel are discriminatory.

## SEXUAL HARASSMENT AND WRONGFUL DISCHARGE

*Sexual harassment* is a high-profile workplace issue and falls within the jurisdiction of Title VII of the Civil Rights Act of 1964, mentioned earlier in this chapter. In 2004, 13,136 complaints were filed with the EEOC charging sexual harassment; 15 percent of them were filed by men. Upon investigation, fewer than half of them were found to have "no reasonable cause."

Sexual harassment is a type of sex discrimination, generally defined as unwanted sexually oriented verbal or physical behavior that makes someone feel uncomfortable or intimidated in the workplace by focusing on a worker's gender rather than his or her professional qualifications.

It applies to men and women, adults, and children, and it includes same-gender harassment.

There are several types of sexual harassment recognized by the courts:

- *Quid pro quo* sexual harassment occurs when a worker's rejection of (or submission to) sexual advances or behavior by a higher-ranking worker or manager is used as a condition of employment, or to make job-related decisions affecting the worker—reassignment, being passed over for promotion, and so on. Generally, only managers can be charged with this type of harassment, because only they can directly affect the pay, benefits, and employment of the worker.[9]
- *Hostile environment* sexual harassment occurs when the unwelcome advances or other behavior create an intimidating or hostile work environment, or when they unreasonably interfere with a worker's job performance. (In this case, the conduct doesn't have to be causing adverse economic effects on the person being harassed.) Unlike quid pro quo harassment, hostile environment harassment can be committed by clients, coworkers, and/or customers as well as by supervisory personnel. Examples of hostile environment sexual harassment include sexually based language, jokes, cartoons, photos, posters, or written materials; fondling; or other unwelcome physical contact. However, there must be a pattern of behavior, not an isolated incident.[10]
- *Third-party* sexual harassment means that workers who were not the specific target of the harassment file claims for quid pro quo or hostile environment sexual harassment because of its overall impact on them.

All companies and organizations with more than 15 employees are required by the Equal Employment Opportunity Commission (EEOC) to create and disseminate a sexual harassment policy and to train employees to understand the issue. Most states also have sexual harassment laws, some of which may be even stricter than federal rules.[11]

The Supreme Court ruled in 1998 that "employers must be proactive in order to avoid a sexual harassment lawsuit." They can no longer use ignorance of a supervisor's or coworker's conduct as a defense against a claim. The Supreme Court also set a two-part standard companies must meet in order to defend themselves from sexual harassment liability:

1. The company made reasonable efforts to prevent and/or correct any sexually harassing behavior in the workplace.
2. The worker being harassed unreasonably failed to exercise any preventive or corrective mechanisms provided by the company.

The best way for managers to avoid sexual harassment claims against them or their companies is to ensure that their personal conduct

## SEXUAL HARASSMENT: POLICIES AND PROCEDURES

A good sexual harassment prevention policy should include the following:

- Definition of harassment

- Harassment prohibition statement

- Complaint procedure description

- Disciplinary process and penalties

- Protection against retaliation statement

A good sexual harassment prevention procedure should include the following:

- Conducting yearly or biannual sexual harassment policy reviews with executive and supervisory personnel

- Investigating worker complaints promptly and thoroughly

- Handling same-sex harassment complaints the same different-gender complaints are handled

- Documenting all results of every sexual harassment complaint or investigation

- Telling employees it is their duty to report all sexual harassment they see or experience

is above reproach, that their company's sexual harassment policy is clearly stated in writing, and that all prospective, new, and current employees not only sign off on the policy but receive periodic reviews of it.

## A Word about Bantering, Flirting, and Teasing

One reason sexual harassment is such a management minefield is that "nature happens" when men and women work together. Bantering, flirting, and teasing are inevitable in almost every workplace, even those that expressly forbid romantic relationships between workers. Another reason is differences in company culture—conduct that may fall comfortably below the threshold of sexual harassment in one workplace can seriously exceed it at another. At the same time, the law allows for a lot of leeway when it comes to bantering, flirting, and teasing—and that leaves a lot of room for potential misunderstandings and misinterpretations.

Title VII of the Civil Rights Act is not a general civility code, and it does not prohibit "genuine but innocuous differences in the ways men and women routinely interact with members of the same sex and of the opposite sex." The Supreme Court's opinions also stress that "simple teasing," gender-related jokes, periodic bad language, and other generally nonrecurring conduct in response to "the ordinary tribulations of the workplace" do not amount to sexual harassment as defined by statute.

The bottom line for employers: The law focuses on what a reasonable person would find abusive, coercive, or unmistakably hostile. However, since the definition of "reasonable" varies from place to place (and court to court), it's better to err on the side of caution when defining a company's internal conduct standards.[12]

## Sexual Preference Discrimination

Openly homosexual or bisexual workers are becoming more commonplace in the United States, and discrimination against workers on the basis of sexual preference can result in lawsuits and other workplace complaints against companies that practice it. Discrimination based on sexual orientation is different from either sex discrimination or sexual harassment. At this writing, there are no federal laws that specifically address workplace discrimination against gays or lesbians for private-sector businesses, so perhaps it is ironic that federal government workers are the only ones legally protected against such discrimination. However, more than 100 cities and counties and more than a dozen states have antidiscrimination laws that include sexual orientation. One clearinghouse for the latest information in this area of law is the Lambda Legal Defense Fund, a group that maintains a list of laws by state.[13] Most deal with the subject somewhat indirectly; the majority of court challenges are based more on the First, Fifth, and Fourteenth Amendments to the U.S. Constitution.

Title VII of the 1964 Civil Rights Act does not cover sexual preference discrimination, nor does the Rehabilitation Act of 1973. The Federal Labor Relations Board, on the other hand, has ruled that because a federal agency "is not required by law to refrain from discrimination based on sexual orientation . . . does not mean the agency cannot agree to refrain from such discrimination."[14]

At the same time, there are still states with laws against homosexuality or same-sex marriage, so sexual preference discrimination claims in those states don't do very well. In 1993, Georgia was one of those states, so the Georgia Department of Law was found not liable when it withdrew a job offer to a woman after learning she planned to marry another woman.[15]

Against this uncertain legal picture, it is important for companies to have written policies regarding sexual preference—both in terms of hiring and offering benefits to same-sex partners of employees—that have been carefully reviewed and approved by attorneys well acquainted with the areas of social and labor law.

## Wrongful Discharge

*Wrongful discharge* is a workplace issue that collides with the long-followed common-law doctrine of employment-at-will, meaning that employees were free to quit their jobs "at will," or at any time—and employers were equally free to discharge employees "at will."

This area of law has become so touchy that most employers must now be very careful about discharging employees for any reason. To protect themselves for wrongful discharge lawsuits, most companies now have detailed dismissal procedures in writing. It is also the reason most companies have a system of regular, written job reviews and other job performance documentation in an employee's file—all to ensure that there are documented "business-related" reasons for discharging the person. Even greater precautions must be taken when the worker is part of a protected class—women, minorities, disabled persons, workers older than 40, and so on.

## CHAPTER SUMMARY

It should be evident by now that there's a lot more to managing a retail business than deciding how to price the merchandise and hiring friendly people to help sell it! This chapter has been an attempt to summarize the major employment-related laws and how they impact company owners and managers, and every employee—from underage part-timers, to new hires, to those who are almost retired.

When seen as a whole, the aim of federal laws appears to be to protect the working public by ensuring that hourly employees are paid a minimum wage, that children don't work in dangerous situations, that workplaces are safe, and that no one is discriminated against in pursuit of jobs they are qualified and willing to perform, to name a few. Critics charge that there are loopholes in many of the laws, and too few federal investigators to uphold their intent or look into any but the most serious or blatant complaints.

From an employer's standpoint, the result of all these laws and enforcement agencies is that every decision that impacts a workforce must be made carefully, administered fairly, and justified legally.

## DISCUSSION QUESTIONS

1. Why would a company have a wage and hour audit performed by a third party?
2. What was the purpose of enacting the Social Security Act? In your opinion, how well does it serve that purpose today?
3. Find out more about the SSA's mismatch letters and what to do if, as an employer or store manager, you receive one.
4. What are the differences between the Civil Rights Acts of 1964 and 1991? Why did Congress decide we needed two of them?
5. How would you write a policy that addresses "less serious" forms of sexual harassment, such as banter and teasing, as well as more blatant incidents? Give it a try, with the intent of sending a clear message to a retail workforce about acceptable (and unacceptable) behavior.

## ENDNOTES

1. Beth Schroeder, "Beware the Class-Action Lawsuit Headed Your Way!" in *Food for Thought*, a newsletter of the Silver & Freedman Employment Law Department, Los Angeles, California, August 2001.
2. Speech by John Henshaw, Occupational Safety & Health Administration, U.S. Department of Labor, to the International Mass Retail Association, Washington, D.C., March 12, 2003.
3. Annual enforcement statistics for FY 2003, Employee Benefits Security Administration, U.S. Department of Labor, Washington, D.C., November 2003.
4. All statistics about EEOC cases throughout this chapter are from the U.S. Equal Employment Opportunity Commission, Washington, D.C.
5. Carol Entelisano, "The Woes of Wal-Mart," Tanner & Guin, LLC, Tuscaloosa, Alabama, on Web site FindLaw.com, February 2005.
6. *What You Should Know about Age Discrimination in the Workplace*, Mansfield, Tanick, and Cohen, P.A., Minneapolis, Minnesota, ©2000.
7. Stephanie Armour, "Pregnant Workers Report Growing Discrimination," *USA Today*, February 16, 2005.
8. Peter Leichtfuss, "ADA Issues Affecting Retailers," Davis Wright Tremaine, LLP, Portland, Oregon, on Web site FindLaw.com, February 2005.

9. "Who Can Engage in 'Quid Pro Quo' Sexual Harassment?" Employment Law section on Web site FreeAdvice.com.

10. "What Are Some Examples of 'Hostile Work Environment' Sexual Harassment?" Employment Law section on Web site FreeAdvice.com.

11. Nancy Wyatt, "What If . . . : Information on Sexual Harassment," Penn State University, University Park, Pennsylvania, 2000.

12. "What about Teasing?" Employment Law section of Web site FreeAdvice.com.

13. *Discrimination Based on Sexual Orientation*, Nolo, Berkeley, California, ©2005.

14. Cited in court decision *Norton v. Macy*, 417 F. 2nd 1161, Circuit Court, Washington, D.C., 1969.

15. Cited in court decision *Shahar v. Bowers,* 836 F. Supp. 859, N.D. Georgia, 1993.

# 3

# MANAGING
# PEOPLE
# EFFECTIVELY

Now our focus shifts from the cut-and-dried requirements of federal employment law to the art, science, and psychology of managing the actual human beings in a workforce.

As we all know, relationships are not unilateral. They involve and demand mutual effort, mutual respect, and mutual concern. There's no way to build enduring customer relationships without competent employees who are personally committed to caring about these relationships. Achieving this level of commitment with employees requires a workforce in which each individual is as motivated to provide these relationships as the individual customers are to enjoy their benefits.

How does a manager achieve this? This chapter focuses on:

- Assigning accountability to employees
- Fostering cooperation among coworkers
- The pitfalls of internal competition
- Eliminating a "caste system" company hierarchy

Learning to compete in a world where every offering must be personalized and unique requires that people in companies learn to think and act differently than many do today. The challenge of the digital age is not so much to improve the value chain, but to reinvent it. Creating the fast, flexible, adaptive, customer-centric organization that has been described in the past is quickly becoming a prerequisite for survival in the future—and it begins with employees who can meet the challenge.

## THE ACCOUNTABILITY DILEMMA

Of the many ways organizations try to improve the performance of their employees, increasing their accountability is one of the most important. In most cases, if people are accountable for what they do, they'll do it better. Accountability can help provide focus, communicate priorities, indicate serious commitment to an issue, create a sense of urgency and tension, and demonstrate to all those in the organization that its leaders are evenhanded and fair. In addition, and perhaps most significantly, studies indicate that accountability may be the single most important factor in effective decision-making. It is hardly a surprise that people who have to live with the consequences of their decisions tend to make better ones.

However, the wrong kind of accountability can focus energy on the wrong kinds of activities and can lead to the formation of bad business habits. For example, it is common for many managers to be largely accountable for what amounts to pleasing their bosses . . . or making those bosses look good to *their* bosses. A manager who is asked to make short-term improvements without regard to the long-term goals of the department or company ends up meeting goals—but perhaps the wrong goals, or for the wrong reasons.

Left unchanged, these accountability practices wed us to the past. They make it more rewarding (or at least, less punishing) to do things as they have always been done. To provide people with a challenging role in a changing organization, accountability must be "designed" so that it supports and encourages that change. The focus needs to be less on immediate (and sometimes meaningless) results and more on continuous (even unreasonable) improvement and learning. As legendary UCLA basketball coach John Wooden advised, "Don't measure yourself by what you have accomplished, but by what you should have accomplished with your ability."

In retail, frontline employees are often asked by their managers to be accountable for their performance when, in fact, these employees have been given little control over the process that they're being held accountable for. Let's take a floor salesperson, for instance, in an upscale department store. Yes, she sells clothing and generally does a good job meeting her sales quota. But if she has no input at all in what goods are purchased by the retail buyer, or how they are priced or displayed, even if she's an incredible salesperson, exactly how much accountability can she truly have? If things aren't selling quickly enough, who is at fault? Does anyone listen to her suggestions, or does she simply learn not to bother making them? This kind of situation can lead to a disheartened workforce and a sales staff that is all too happy to relate their troubles to customers. It is also unfair to hold employees accountable for something they can't do, don't control, or can't change.

How can this mismatch be averted? There are three questions a manager should ask before assigning accountability:

1. **What must be done?** Before people can be held accountable, they must understand what they are being held accountable for—and they shouldn't be held accountable for performing an activity, but for making a significant contribution to the particular task or area. Also, more frequently than anyone wants to admit, people are held accountable for tasks not worth performing. Every task for which an individual is to be held accountable must be examined to ensure that it adds value. If a task is not worth doing, don't hold anyone accountable for doing it. In fact, stop doing it!

2. **Who will be accountable?** Who's responsible? Is it a person, or a group? Too often, lines of responsibility are unclear. Accountability should be assigned at the lowest possible level in the store's hierarchy. Those closest to the customers (or the processes) are best

equipped to deal with them and should, therefore, be the ones who are held accountable for doing so. Where there are teams, there should be team—not individual—accountability. Team members must win or lose as a team. When the question is asked, "Who's accountable here?" there should be a single raised hand on behalf of the team—not a half-dozen fingers pointing in every direction.

3. **What abilities will those being held accountable need to achieve success?** The issues raised by this question are often discussed but rarely resolved. There are very few systematic plans in retail businesses to ensure that the right people in the process have sufficient control, or the right skills, to do the job required. This problem is sometimes compounded by a managerial mind-set that often results in managers receiving the lion's share of the benefits of training and education.

## Shifting the Balance of Power

Most organizations work from the assumption that management knows best—that managers ought to have control until a convincing argument can be made to the contrary. If lower-level employees (or teams) seek greater authority, they must ask for it, and then demonstrate that they deserve it and will use it wisely, and—maybe most important—they must show that transferring the authority will lead to a preferable result. The burden of proof, in other words, lies with the employees.

What if that burden was shifted to management? In this paradigm, the assumption would be that the people (or more likely, teams) who work the process also have complete authority over it and are held accountable for its success. Meanwhile, if anyone wants to centralize authority (i.e., move authority farther up the hierarchy, assuming there is one), he or she will have to convince the organization that this would lead to a preferable outcome. It would also be up to the team to ask for the help it needed, submit its own budgets, measure its own performance, calculate its return on investment to the company, and generally justify that it is worthy of its members' salaries and the organization's decision to entrust it with ownership of the process.

Shifting the burden of proof in this manner represents a major shift in the role of management in most organizations. While incorporating "empowered" teams into a traditional environment is a significant task, shifting the burden of proof is an even greater challenge. It demands entirely different accountability practices and an entirely different environment. Still, giving people the type of knee-knocking accountability that

## THE CASE OF THE NONPERFORMING WHALES—PART ONE

A colleague of ours visited the pool where killer whales are trained at a large amusement park. When the trainer asked if anyone knew how killer whales were trained, our colleague raised his hand.

"You feed them a few of the fish when they do well, and when they don't do well, they don't get the fish."

When he saw the trainer smile, he knew that he was in trouble and wished that he could take his words back. No such luck!

"You mean you want me to punish them—not feed the nonperformers, make sure the whales are good and hungry, and then get into the tank and swim with them? I don't think I want to be part of that experiment, thank you very much!" said the trainer.

Whales have to be fed. You can't train them if they are preoccupied with their hunger (lower-level needs). That was an important lesson.

With people, as with whales, we can learn only when we are not preoccupied with our survival and security. The good news with whales is that such a strategy is life-threatening. Unfortunately, with people, we manipulate them, using the organizational equivalent of the fish without fear of immediate harm. The result is that we do not feel the need to find a better way.

puts them at risk—the way that the business's owners are at risk—is an effective alternative to a system that boasts empowerment but often delivers a great deal less.

Ralph Stayer, a former CEO of Johnsonville Foods, was asked once about team training. "Mostly unnecessary," he replied. "Just give people a real job, and the team will form and work effectively." When the responsibility is there, when the authority is "real," and when people have job competency, they will do what they have to do to deliver the value they are being held accountable for.

## COOPERATION VS. COMPETITION

Teamwork—we're all for it! Or are we? Many companies pay big bucks to sign their employees up for team-building exercises. They get together for a retreat that includes climbing rope ladders, rafting rivers, facing mythical enemies, or solving mysteries. Over and over, people are told they "have to learn to work together more effectively," and for good reason. Today's world is too complex for any one person to create value in her workplace by herself. This is especially true for companies in which individuals from different functional areas, departments, and physical locations have to work in harmony to meet the unique needs of their customers. If we hope to succeed in the retail industry, there is no real alternative for many of us but to work as a team, to cooperate.

However, it is this alternative that most organizations are least well equipped to implement. We are simply not prepared to cooperate—culturally, structurally, or philosophically. We are, after all, a nation that makes heroes of individuals who distinguish themselves competitively. From corporate raiders to rock stars, from baseball's Most Valuable Player to the most famous heart surgeon, we've focused on individual winners. Looking out for Number One is not only expected but is rewarded.

Nowhere is winning (and losing) more a part of everyday life than in our organizations. So companies talk about teamwork, but their internal systems don't reward it, our corporate culture doesn't support it, and our leaders are reluctant to embrace it. People return from their team-building weekends, and within a few days (or hours), they're often back to building their empires at the expense of the other person and with the hope of a superior (i.e., winning) performance appraisal, higher merit pay, the next promotion, or more job security. To meet today's demands, we need to be pulling together, yet the internal competition endemic to our system is undermining our efforts.

## The Hidden Costs of Competition

This is not to say that cooperation doesn't exist in most organizations. People frequently act on their more noble instincts and help one another. Indeed, it is nothing less than amazing that, given the systemic promotion of competition and the resistance to cooperation, there is as much pulling together as there is. It seems that individuals are genuinely driven to do the "right thing"—contributing to the overall good of the organization—rather than feathering their own nests. But the cards in many companies are essentially stacked against it. There are simply too many barriers to acting decently and cooperatively and, conversely, too many rewards for acting otherwise. Ironically, what is scarce and often bitterly fought for in the corporation (e.g., the boss's praise, the "Employee of the Month" parking space) is not even necessarily something that has real value in the outside world.

What are the potential downside risks to this behavior? We can think of eight, for starters:

1. **Internal competition squashes creativity and innovation.** Individuals competing against one another must be playing the same, or similar, game so that the appropriate comparisons can be made and the winners selected—which makes it more difficult for the individual competitor to experiment and try new methods. The result can be significantly lower levels of creativity and innovation.

2. **Internal competition inhibits dialogue.** Add the concept of winning and losing to a dialogue and you get a debate. In an internally competitive environment, individuals become less interested in sharing and thinking about new or conflicting information and become more concerned with scoring points or pressing their case, right or wrong.

3. **Internal competition can negatively impact relationships.** Though many of us naturally expect the best from people, when we know we are competing—whether for a promotion, to curry favor with the boss, or to get a bonus—it is difficult for us to build trust, work as a team member, or create an honest relationship. Competition makes people suspicious of one another and often results in greater anxiety in employees, who constantly feel they have to watch their backs.

4. **Internal competition lowers product and service quality.** As different individuals and departments compete, the temptation may be to cut corners to get products and services out as quickly and profitably as possible—particularly if the problems created aren't major enough to become big problems.

5. **Internal competition destroys focus.** "Winning" and "process or product improvement" are very different goals. When people compete with a focus on winning, they often take the fastest, most reliable, most predictable route to winning—which is rarely the most effective route to continually improving the method of work.

6. **Internal competitiveness reduces efficiency.** When individuals are less innovative, less trusting, or more combative, it costs the company in a variety of ways. For example, when people compete with one another, they tend to work independently. They may not realize they are duplicating the efforts of others, or generating data for projects for which perfectly good data already exist.

7. **Internal competition demotivates those who don't win.** The theory was that if people competed and the winners were rewarded, they would feel appreciated and all those who didn't win would strive to do so in the future. In most cases, however, it hasn't worked out that way. Far too many ill-thought-out and incomplete reward systems

have resulted in the selection of "winners" whose performance was not any better, and was sometimes objectively worse, than that of some of the "losers." Predictably, this can be demotivating to those who "lose"—but this is hard to quantify, because our companies evaluate motivational effectiveness by tracking the reactions of the winners rather than the nonwinners.

8. **Internal competition lessens self-esteem.** When some people lose, they begin to question their ability to succeed in this (and maybe any other) system. After all, they worked hard, tried their best, and came up short. Remember, losing is more common than winning, because the system has been designed to ensure that most people don't win. The long-term effect of constantly coming up short can be significant. Less confident people simply don't learn or experiment as effectively as confident people.

## BUILDING COOPERATION

There are many ways a good manager can break the hold that internal competition may have on a retail organization:

- **Increase the interactions between individuals and groups.** The faceless person in another department or store who performs another function can easily be ignored. It is easier to cooperate with people you know, especially if the interaction is frequent and you have to cooperate to get a job done.

- **Ensure that everyone has the opportunity to win.** This doesn't mean rewarding nonperformers. However, when several people seek the same goal and the number of "wins" is artificially limited, competition will result. If everyone can win, one person's success doesn't necessitate another's failure.

- **Establish cooperation and respect as core values.** As long as internal competition is tolerated, little will change. Elevating cooperation to a core value will ensure that climbing someone else's back to get ahead will be career-limiting. Take a few minutes to analyze whether cooperation has been career-enhancing in the organizations for which you have worked. How did you know whether people were cooperating effectively? What happened to people in the organization who played politics at the expense of others?

- **Educate everyone about the entire process.** If people understand how their performance affects others, they will be less likely to act in ways that negatively impact others or the company. Most people want to do the right thing and, given a choice, will make a good decision unless it is personally punishing. Providing information about the process enables each person to make an informed choice.

- **A focus on short-term results often leads to a less cooperative environment.** If a person has only a short time in which to impress the boss or make an impact, the long-term benefits of cooperation can be perceived to be less important. This is especially true if a person will be rotated off of a project or out of a department before he or she experiences the negative effects of noncooperation.

- **If part of everyone's evaluation included an analysis of what a person or group had done to further teamwork, most organizations would be very different.** As a manager, make it a point to ask your employees: Whom have you helped lately? From whom have you learned? What have you taught to a coworker? What kinds of training would help your group as a whole? Who else in the company has influenced your thinking the most? Which people, outside your group or department, have been the most instrumental in helping you succeed?

- **Involve everyone in at least one cross-functional improvement effort.** Mandating that people must work beyond the boundaries of their own department or functional area will result not only in more talent being applied to complicated process issues, but also in a greater appreciation of how the entire process works *to benefit the customer.* One of the most important reasons to mandate participation may be symbolic, showing people that cooperation is not optional and that everyone will actively participate. People should also be held accountable for their participation—there's no greater waste of time than to be a "mandated" team member on a team that accomplishes very little.

- **Consider teams as the primary unit of responsibility.** Design-in interdependence. It hardly makes sense for several members on the team to be able to win when the team as a whole loses, or when the customer is shortchanged. If a task requires teamwork, ensure that teamwork is required of everyone. Make the team responsible and accountable.

An important caveat: As some organizations have begun to organize in teams, many have been unwilling to abandon the old structure completely, keeping team members accountable as individuals to their former functional department. The result is usually a group that does not function as a team but as individuals representing an area of expertise, each with veto power over most decisions. Frustration levels tend to be high as people are torn between functional responsibilities and group commitments. If we want teams to act like teams, we must make them

## THE CASE OF THE NONPERFORMING WHALES—PART TWO

There must be times when a killer whale just doesn't want to learn, no matter how many fish it has consumed. So our colleague asked what they did when they identified a problem whale.

"We fire it," he was told. "I mean, it's probably a good whale but just not right for our whale show. So we let it go—that is, if we can't get our competition to take the whale from us.

"We don't make that decision easily," the trainer continued. "It's expensive to find another whale, so we first ensure that we are not the problem. And at some point, if our efforts don't succeed, we just have to cut our losses. Otherwise, it would cost $75 for the show—$30 to see the performing whales, and $45 to help us feed the whales in the pool out back, where we keep the nonperformers. And heaven help us if the 'performers' ever found out they could get the same treatment out back, without working!"

cohesive units, with a real task and team accountability. "Going halfway" can be very costly.

## THE WORKPLACE "CASTE SYSTEM"

In many organizations today, a large number of employees are given the not-so-subtle message that they should "know their place." Retail firms are no exception. For many, there is little in the work environment that encourages them to reinvent the way work is done or to invent new roles for themselves. Often, the exact opposite is communicated. People are taught that bucking the system can be career-limiting, and that obedience and being perceived as a good team player are all-important. They are expected to learn their roles quickly and not to venture too far onto someone else's turf.

In traditional, command-and-control business structures, different treatment of different "classes" of employees was at the heart of maintaining order in the hierarchy. The costly by-product of these practices has been reduced flexibility, less learning, and an increased feeling of helplessness among certain groups. History and common sense tell us that we are healthier and more productive when we resist the instinct (natural or otherwise) to set ourselves apart from those with whom we work.

Providing inspiration and impetus for the past successes of many of our leaders has often been the distinctly American notion that anyone can be anything he or she wants to be, that anyone can grow up to be president. Where a person was born, or how humble his or her upbringing, are regarded as not critical to the person's eventual success in this country as opposed to in others. After all, America was built by men and women who transcended their past and believed they could "dream big"—and change their fate. Our recent entrepreneurial history suggests that this dream is still alive for many. However, for a growing number of people locked in certain jobs (particularly in service-sector jobs, like retail salespeople and cashiers), the American dream is just that—a dream. Where you went to school, if you went to school, where you entered the organization, whom you worked for, and which department trained you can brand you and greatly influence your ability to grow and succeed.

The unfortunate fact is that the first impression a person gives may make or break his or her career in many companies. We've all either been there or seen it happen: The boss who takes a liking to us gives us more responsibility, treats us as an important team member, delegates decision-making responsibility, and works hard to ensure that we are supported. The not-so-subtle communication is that we've been "selected" as a top performer, and not surprisingly, we often succeed. Even if we fail along the way, the person who "marked us for success" has a vested interest in ensuring that his or her judgment was correct and bails us out.

On the other hand, we have all seen what can happen when people are branded with less favorable endorsements. They get less interesting duties, worse hours on the schedule, less responsibility, less decision-making authority, and less positive support. For some employees, the result seems inevitable. They are treated as part of the underclass, and success is substantially more difficult for them to achieve. Little wonder that, as we learned in Chapter 2, the U.S. Equal Employment Opportunity Commission receives more than 150,000 complaints a year from workers charging some form of discrimination. Imagine the ones who have similar complaints but *don't* file them with a federal agency, and it is clear that some percentage of American workers feel disenfranchised.

While some of the messages about our status are subtle, many are often explicit and unambiguous. In a big corporation, try eating in the executive dining room if you're not one of the executives. In the same building, could a newcomer tell who has more power by where and how big their office is? By what is hanging on their walls? By the quality of their office furnishings?

The full effect of the subtle (and often not-so-subtle) messages created as a by-product of treating people differently within an organization is sometimes not readily apparent to those who work there. If, however, we can step back far enough to get an objective view, it becomes quickly evident that the unintended caste system that has evolved undermines our ability to capture the potential of the workforce. Class distinctions tend to create bureaucracy, lessen self-esteem, and lead to a feeling in many individuals that they have little control over the systems in which they work.

Downsizing and flattening organizational hierarchies might help cut down on the negative effects of class distinctions, but if companies don't change the structures that created the problems initially, it won't be long before a similar caste system emerges.

David B. Wright, an executive vice president of EMC Corporation—a company with more than 23,000 employees and sales that top $8 billion—has made this observation: "One of the things I believe causes problems in business is that we don't realize that knowledge has nothing to do with organization structure. Therefore, people can be smarter than you at a certain thing. Just because they work two or three levels below you in the organization, or work differently, doesn't mean that you should ignore their knowledge. We really have a problem with that in organizations. We are so much in the information age that it used to be knowledge is power. Now knowledge is everywhere. If you try to be the knowledge power broker today, you will die in the marketplace."

The good news is that, in organizations where things have to get done quickly, people have less time for, and less patience with, the trappings of status. In these organizations, the demonstrated ability to contribute is everything, and class and status are next to nothing. The challenge, then, is for each of us to choose to make it increasingly difficult to differentiate unfairly, or unnecessarily, among our fellow employees.

## CHAPTER SUMMARY

This chapter discussed three of the most common problems in businesses today, each of which is often left to managers to either solve or live with. The first issue is how to make people accountable for their work and the results thereof. All too often, "accountability" is a catchphrase. This chapter discussed the merits of breaking down the process into manageable steps: Determine who is accountable, and for exactly what. Don't make people "accountable" for something they have no control over. Don't assign accountability for mundane tasks just to make people feel that their busywork is important when it's not. Find out what kinds of training a worker needs in order to really make progress in the areas for which he or she is accountable.

The next issue is motivating workers without forcing them to compete against each other. The authors feel strongly that old-style "motivational" systems—constant comparison of results and pitting employees or teams against each other in a race for a prize or award—often backfire. These tactics make people more likely to cut corners, less likely to trust one another, and even less creative in the long run. A number of suggestions were discussed to take the focus off competition and put it on cooperation.

Finally, the chapter discussed the all-too-common corporate trap of treating different levels of employees differently—executives, midlevel managers, administrative assistants, and the like. Many companies unwittingly send subtle messages about the "haves" and "have-nots" in their ranks. What does this say to the have-nots? Managers and employees alike are cautioned to ignore the trappings of status and deal with coworkers as intelligent equals, and to expect the same treatment in return.

## DISCUSSION QUESTIONS

1. In your own work life, past or present, describe an example of someone being held accountable for a task that (in your opinion) should not be done at all, or—even if it must be done—isn't important enough to assign personal accountability for it. Why do you think it was done that way? How would you change the rules?
2. What are the costs of internal competition in a retail company? Name and describe at least three of them.
3. How would you as a manager design a system that rewards high-sales performers without having a negative impact on the rest of the employees?
4. How would you describe the typical retail employee's ideal balance between feeling independent and accountable while also working as a team member?
5. Without the "perks" of being a senior executive in a "caste system" organization, would people still want to be executives at all? Shouldn't people who have worked hard enjoy the benefits of "life at the top" of their companies? Discuss your opinions with the class.

4

# MANAGING UNION EMPLOYEES

The percentage of workers in the United States who are members of labor unions has declined steadily since the 1960s, when "union density" averaged 30 percent. Today, it averages 13 percent.[1] Nevertheless, dealing with unions and their employees are big parts of retail management because unions associated with retail exert considerable influence, and compliance with union-related rules and regulations can be a challenge for managers who are unfamiliar with labor union hierarchy and terminology.

In this chapter, you will learn about:

- The size, scope, and philosophies of the primary unions associated with retail workers
- How unions are structured and organized
- Union representatives' roles in the workplace
- Grievance procedures in unionized workplaces
- How managers should interact with union employees and union representatives

Today, more than 16 million Americans belong to scores of different unions, all of which seek better wages, working conditions, and benefits for their members.[2] Workers join unions for the same basic reasons that people join groups of all kinds: safety in numbers, collective bargaining power, and a sense of belonging. Many unions have also done an excellent job of providing ongoing training for their people, for skilled tasks that may be difficult to find in the general labor pool.

## A BRIEF HISTORY OF LABOR UNIONS

Before the Industrial Revolution (1740 to 1830), associations of skilled workers were known as "craftsmen guilds" that set up professional standards and apprenticeship systems for their members. During the early decades of the Industrial Revolution, English craftsmen guilds evolved into the unions with which we are familiar today. Workers organized to protect their members from abuse, overwork, and poor pay at the hands of industrialists who viewed workers as another piece of their machinery.

It took more than a century, however, before unions gained any serious ability to reduce 12- to 14-hour workdays in dangerous factories for low wages, or limit pervasive company use of child labor. During the first decades of the twentieth century, however, unions grew enormously in size, power, and influence. The United Steel Workers of America, for example, started organizing in 1936 and within six years grew to include more than 700,000 members in the United States and Canada.[3]

Unions also served as a center of social and community activity, particularly in "company towns," the small settlements that sprang up around mills and mines and existed solely to provide housing for a company's workers. Camaraderie and togetherness are a natural result of individuals working together, and these were key precepts of union organizers, who often emphasized this point by calling their organizations "brotherhoods" and "fraternal orders." Union halls were often the hubs of nonunion and social activities because in many company towns and even in larger towns and cities, there was no other place outside of churches for large groups of workers to congregate.

Today, many of these primary reasons for joining unions have been diluted because government legislation and judicial oversight over the years have become the primary protectors of workers' rights, and because there are more social groups and associations today that workers can join to achieve the sense of belonging. However, the average union employee makes 25 percent more each week than the average nonunion employee in the same job category—reason enough to make union membership attractive to many.[4]

Historically, employers that have resisted the unionization of their workforces have done so for two reasons:

- It interferes with management's ability to run the company as its owners see fit.
- It introduces an "outsider" element to the employer-employee relationship and can divide workers' loyalties between company and union.

When a company is unionized, it must subscribe to union-dictated work rules, pay scales, job protection procedures, and other union policies that often affect its business processes to the point that costs increase and profits decrease.

Employers also prefer straightforward manager-to-employee communications; they don't like the basic union feature of the union **shop steward**, the on-site employee who serves as the union representative and may become involved in even the most minor disputes or misunderstandings between managers and other employees.

## TYPES OF UNIONS

Unions today take two basic forms—craft and industrial. **Craft unions** were the foundation organizations of the union movement. Like guilds before them, they focus on workers with similar skills doing similar jobs, and generally include apprenticeship programs among their functions. Actors, boilermakers, carpenters, electricians, ironworkers, machinists, plumbers, railway engineers, and stoneworkers are among the skill sets represented by craft unions.

Craft unions exert their power through the ability to control the labor supply of a given craft. They are strongest at the local level.

**Industrial unions** are associations made up of all workers in a single industry. These workers perform different jobs requiring different skills and skill levels, including many that are represented by craft unions. Autoworkers, mine workers, steelworkers, and textile workers are among the industries represented by industrial unions, which exert their power primarily through the ability to control the labor supply of a given industry. They are strongest at the national level.

Up until 1955, craft unions belonged to the American Federation of Labor and industrial unions were organized into the Congress of Industrial Organizations. They merged in that year to form the American Federation of Labor-Congress of Industrial Organizations, better known today by its acronym, AFL-CIO. The AFL-CIO represents members of 58 separate unions.

In addition to the AFL-CIO, there are several unions with which retail managers may have to deal directly, and several others that (at least indirectly) affect the management of retail businesses. Here's a brief look at some of the major ones:

- **UNITE HERE** represents 450,000 workers in apparel and textile manufacturing, apparel distribution centers, apparel retail, industrial laundries, hotels, casinos, food service, airport concessions, and restaurants. This union resulted from the 2004 merger of the Union of Needletrades, Textiles and Industrial Employees (UNITE) with the Hotel Employees and Restaurant Employees International (HERE).[5] Originally, UNITE itself was also the result of a merger—the joining in 1995 of the once-powerful International Ladies Garment Workers Union (ILGWU) and the Amalgamated Clothing and Textile Workers' Union. Some of the companies whose workers belong to UNITE HERE include Aramark, Brooks Brothers, Caesar's Entertainment, Harrah's Entertainment, Hilton, Hyatt, Levi Strauss, Liz Claiborne, MGM-Mirage, National Linen, Walt Disney World Company, and Xerox.[6]

- The **Industrial Workers of the World** (IWW) represents several thousand U.S. workers, and others worldwide. It is a small, independent union founded in 1905 that describes itself as being dedicated to "organizing on the job, in our industries and in our communities both to win better conditions today and to build a world without bosses, a world in which production and distribution are organized by workers ourselves to meet the needs of the entire population, not merely a handful of exploiters."[7] Its outspoken Web site explains its system of organizing by company rather than by trade or work niche to improve its bargaining power. An IWW-affiliated union, General Distribution Workers Industrial Union 660, represents all workers in general distribution facilities, and wholesale and retail businesses.

- The **International Brotherhood of Teamsters** (IBT) is one of the best-known and most powerful unions in the United States. It was founded in 1903 and has more than 1.4 million members in 500 local chapters, in occupations that include computer and other technical fields, law and law enforcement, health care, education, transportation, construction, food production, and government service, to name a few. More than half of the IBT's members work in just five areas: freight, industrial trades, parcel, public employees, and warehouse. Most Teamster activity is concentrated in the eastern and midwestern United States.[8]

For the most part, the IBT does not organize retail employees, but retail managers must be aware of this union because so much of a retail company's supply chain is dependent upon Teamster-controlled warehousing and transportation, including package delivery—the United Parcel Service's 200,000 workers are the IBT's largest contingent.

## The AFL-CIO

If your company is unionized, it's important to understand at least the basics about how a union's national organization works. In most cases, it will be the AFL-CIO. Both UNITE HERE and the Teamsters are AFL-CIO-affiliated unions.

The AFL-CIO is the "Congress," of sorts, for 58 unions and more than 13 million of the approximately 16 million union workers in the United States. As a national organization, it does not bargain with company owners—its member unions are autonomous—but it wields enormous influence, setting various member standards, mediating member union disputes, and generally supporting member unions in various ways. The AFL-CIO's stated mission is as follows:

> To improve the lives of working families—to bring economic justice to the workplace and social justice to our nation. To accomplish this mission we will build and change the American labor movement . . . by organizing workers into unions. We will recruit and train the next generation of organizers . . . lead the labor movement in these efforts . . . build a strong political voice for workers . . . change our unions to provide

a new voice to workers in a changing economy . . . speak for working people in the global economy . . . make the voices of working families heard . . . (and) speak out in effective and creative ways on behalf of all working Americans.[9]

The AFL-CIO is governed by 50 state federations and a Puerto Rico federation, in a process that is largely democratic. Elected delegates meet every four years to set general policies and goals and to elect national officers, as well as an Executive Council that is made up of a member of each of its 51 federations. These officers do the AFL-CIO's daily work, which is carried out by 12 departments, including:

- Organizing
- Field Mobilization
- Office of Capital Stewardship
- Investment
- Collective Bargaining
- Legislative
- Political
- Public Policy
- Public Affairs
- Civil, Human, and Women's Rights
- International Affairs
- Safety and Health
- Office of General Counsel

The AFL-CIO also has seven trade and industrial departments:

- Building and Construction Trades
- Food and Allied Service Trades
- Maritime Trades
- Metal Trades
- Professional Employees
- Transportation Trades
- Union Label and Service Trades

In addition to its member unions, the AFL-CIO is allied with a number of other organizations:

- The Housing and Building Investment Trusts
- The Union Privilege
- The National Labor College
- WORKING AMERICA
- The AFL-CIO Working for America
- The International Labor Communications Association

- The Alliance for Retired Americans
- The Center for Working Capital
- The Solidarity Center

Each of the 51 state federations are led by officers and boards elected by state union delegates from each of their local unions; and the state federations coordinate the political and legislative activities of the local unions. This same task is performed at the county and city level by more than 500 *central labor councils*.[10]

## National Union Structure

Each of the unions represented by the AFL-CIO has its own national office and a host of local unions. Since the 1980s, a union's national office generally does not negotiate contracts or involve itself in daily operations or employee-employer relationships. Instead, like the AFL-CIO, the national offices organize new workers to expand the union membership and support their member locals in a variety of ways. Unlike the AFL-CIO, however, the national union offices control the union's financial resources—strike funds, campaign contributions, and other operating funds. This is a significant change from the mid–twentieth century, when union national offices did the primary contract bargaining, leaving local unions to negotiate only relatively minor issues related to specific regions or companies. The "old" chain of command is shown in Figure 4-1.

Since the mid-1980s, however, bargaining has decentralized, in large part because of industry decentralization, and globalization. Today, most major bargaining is done by local unions, and it often focuses more on maintaining jobs rather than preserving union wage and benefit scales. So, as shown in Figure 4-2, while national union offices are

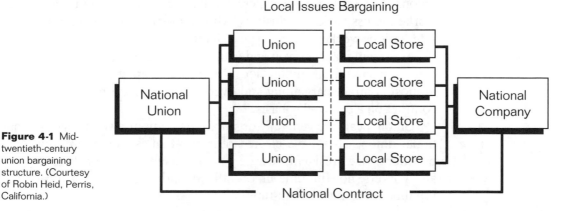

**Figure 4-1** Mid-twentieth-century union bargaining structure. (Courtesy of Robin Heid, Perris, California.)

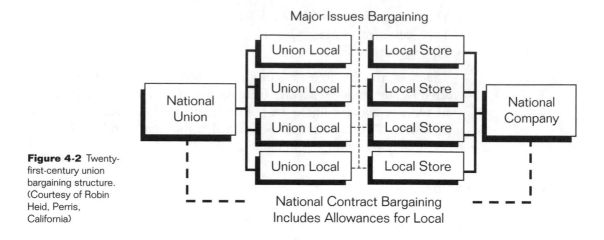

**Figure 4-2** Twenty-first-century union bargaining structure. (Courtesy of Robin Heid, Perris, California)

still involved in contract bargaining, they generally do not control the overall outcome anymore.

## Local Union Structure

Whether contract bargaining is done at the national or local level, among the main union attributes is the safety-in-numbers concept known as **collective bargaining**. This means the union negotiates similar pay for its member workers doing similar jobs, regardless of the industry, company, and/or region in which they work. They do so by pursuing the philosophy of "removing labor from the equation"—basing production costs on differences in managerial and administrative costs, not on labor costs.

Collective bargaining has always been more local union–focused in the craft unions, but more national union–focused in the industrial unions. As mentioned earlier, craft unions tend to represent one type of worker across various industries, while industrial unions tend to represent various workers in one type of industry.

As a retail manager, you and your union employees will have most of your contact with the union "local," the local chapter that takes the lead in most contract bargaining and oversees the provisions of the current contract on a day-to-day basis.

Union locals are generally organized as miniature versions of the national union. They have elected officers—that is, some variation of a president, vice president, secretary, and treasurer. Most of these officers are workers, not full-time union officers, although in larger locals, the top union jobs may be full-time.

Local unions also have a second administrative tier. It consists of a contract administration section made up of worker advocates—called business agents and/or shop stewards—and elected grievance committees to ensure unionized companies operate safely and in accordance with the union contract.

Local industrial unions use **shop stewards** exclusively as on-site contract monitors and grievance handlers. A shop steward is a union member at the workplace, elected by fellow employees to

- Make sure the contract is followed by the company
- Handle grievances by serving as intermediary between employee and supervisor
- Accompany employees anytime they are disciplined by management
- Have copies of the contract with them at all times
- Be accessible to all union members in the workplace
- Notify employers about workplace safety violations

The show steward initiates a grievance process and moves it through the union hierarchy until it's either resolved at a lower level or referred to the local union's grievance committee for a closer look.

In a local craft union, the main contract administrator and grievance handler is the **business agent**. This person works for the union and travels regularly to each worksite within the union's jurisdiction to keep tabs on contract compliance and grievances. A business agent is a local union employee who handles any problems the shop steward cannot, and generally oversees union-employer relations at several job sites.

A craft union business agent usually appoints company workers at various worksites as union stewards to perform some of this work, particularly during the early phases of an employee grievance.[11]

## THE GRIEVANCE PROCESS

When an employee belongs to a union, the employer-employee relationship can be a bit more complicated than with nonunion workers because there's a third-party involved—your company's shop steward or the business agent for the union. Perhaps the most important part of dealing with these worker advocates is understanding what happens when a union member files a complaint, which is called a **grievance**. A grievance is generally defined as an alleged violation by management of the terms, applications, or interpretations of the union contract in effect at the company. A grievance may also be filed if an employee (or worker advocate) claims that the company or manager has violated civil or criminal law.

In most cases, the grievance process is very specific and is spelled out step-by-step in the contract. This is why it's important for managers to be familiar with the union contracts their companies have agreed to. Often, these documents are negotiated by senior management and corporate attorneys—and the day-to-day manager never even reads the document until he or she is faced with a grievance.

The contract is at the heart of almost every grievance, so knowing that contract at least as well as your company's worker advocate does can reduce the number of grievances filed. When you clearly understand the terms, conditions, and applications of the contract, you are less likely to inadvertently violate it.

Managers must also remember that the shop stewards and business managers for their local unions are either union employees or elected by the company's workers. Because of this, they are more likely to err on the side of the worker in a potential grievance, especially in the case of an elected shop steward trying to "please the electorate." When managers know the contract details, they can more easily derail those grievances that clearly fall outside the contract—making it clear to the steward that workers must follow the contract provisions as precisely as management does.

For potentially legitimate grievance filings, the situation is the same—the more managers know about the contract details, the more quickly the situation can be resolved and everyone can get back to work. Perhaps the most important thing for managers to keep in mind is that even if someone has a legitimate complaint, it may not be a topic that is addressed in the union contract with the company. If it doesn't fall within the bounds of the contract, it is *not* a grievance and *does not* belong in the grievance process. In these cases, alternate methods of resolution may be suggested.

Of course, unions know how to play this game, too. Members of a union local in Kansas City, Missouri, post information that urges shop stewards to "know your agreement and use it as creatively as possible to write grievances." While many grievances are violations of the law, some may be based on changes in "past practice"—customary ways of doing things that are perhaps not written into the contract but are largely understood and accepted by both union and company. When an employer tries to change a past practice, it may be seen by union employees as a way of eroding their privileges or benefits, which opens the company to the possibility of a grievance. Grievances may also be the result of discipline-related actions, if a union employee has been disciplined unfairly compared to other workers.[12]

## Investigating a Grievance

Worker advocates usually follow a standardized grievance procedure to determine the basic facts of a grievance, assess its validity and context, and figure out how best to resolve it. The procedural details may vary, but all are based on basic reporting and interviewing skills—skills that should also be used by managers to bring the grievance process at their company to faster, better conclusions.

When the union representative comes to a manager with a grievance, the manager should essentially do with the shop steward, for instance, what the shop steward has already done with the aggrieved employee: pose some key questions. A suggested line of questioning may be as follows:

### Step One: Basic Reporting Questions

1. *Who* is the employee in question?
2. *What* happened?
3. *When* did it happen?
4. *Where* did it happen?
5. *Why* does the employee/union consider it to be a grievance?

### Step Two: Basic Context Questions

1. What does the union say?
2. What happened before in similar situations?
3. What is the grievant's history with the issue?
4. What does the grievant want to settle the issue?

The third step in this process should be a meeting between the manager and the worker advocate. As the manager, here are the steps you should take to get the facts you need, while protecting the rights of your employee, yourself, and the company:

1. **Promptly set a date to meet with the worker advocate.** Be sure to schedule enough time so the worker advocate won't feel rushed and/or think you don't consider the advocate, the employee, or the grievance to be important.
2. ***Listen carefully* before responding.** Let the worker advocate explain the grievance from the employee's and the union's viewpoint, even if the advocate is upset, overly passionate, or makes the issue into a

"political" debate. Make eye contact, get the facts straight, and don't hesitate to go over key points as many times as necessary to establish the circumstances that surround this grievance.

3. **Insist on detail if the worker advocate speaks too generally—** "Everyone does this," or "Everyone says that." Who specifically is "everyone?" What specifically does "everyone" say? Who else will support or attest to the key points made in the grievance?

4. **Keep good notes of the meeting**. Refer to the answers in Steps One and Two to make sure you've covered all the key areas.

5. **Explain your needs to the advocate.** Make it clear that you need the entire grievance details before you can make a good decision about the grievance, or you need to meet with *your* supervisor if a decision falls outside your authority.

6. **Stress the need for honesty.** Be sure the worker advocate understands that if he or she knows something the company doesn't, it can only delay the outcome and maybe even hurt the worker's chances for a satisfactory outcome.

7. **Try to determine the union's position on this issue if it is not clearly stated, or if for any reason the actions of the grievant and/or the worker advocate don't make sense.** If either of these conditions exists, you're probably missing something. You'll need to go over the key points again with the advocate, or perhaps ask more questions. Reiterate that it's important for you to have full details and a clear understanding of the grievance—and the union position on it—in order for you to take the next steps (i.e., respond, pass it on to a supervisor, and so on).

8. **Be well versed in the contract language that pertains to the grievance.** Also research any actions taken in earlier cases involving similar grievances, and anything else that will give you a clearer picture of the strengths and weaknesses of the grievance.

9. **Be clear on what the grievant and the union want done to settle the issue, but never promise a settlement, even when you're sure**

## A DISCIPLINE GRIEVANCE FACT SHEET

The most common form of grievance is initiated after an employee is disciplined. The UNITE HERE union uses the fact sheet shown in Figure 4-3 to process discipline grievances. This fact sheet can serve two purposes for managers: It shows how a union worker advocate will probably think about and respond to a discipline grievance, and it is a good template for a manager's discipline fact sheet.

---

# DISCIPLINE GRIEVANCE FACT SHEET

(This does not go to the company. It is only to be used by the union. Use back if necessary.)

Grievant Name _____ Phone _____

Department _____ Job _____

What discipline was given? _____ Date of discipline _____

1. Did grievant do what he or she was disciplined for? __ Yes __ No __ Unclear

2. Why was the grievant disciplined? What happened? Was there an incident, are there witnesses, who are they and what do they say?

IF THE GRIEVANT DID IT:

3. Are all workers disciplined for breaking this rule, or is there favoritism?

4. Did the worker know about the rule, know the penalty? Is it a new rule or an old rule that was never enforced?

5. Is the rule reasonable for workers to follow? Is it related to safe and efficient operations? Have other workers had problems following this rule?

6. Does the punishment fit the seriousness of the offense and the worker's history?

7. Did the company follow their own rules for discipline, giving the worker a chance to improve? Did the company investigate before issuing discipline? Did they question the worker unfairly? Did they discipline the worker reasonably quickly? Did they give one kind of discipline, then change it?

8. Did the company violate the FMLA (for serious illness of the worker or family)?

9. Do we need copies of company records to see if other workers have been disciplined for breaking this rule? Are there other records that might help?

Steward _____ Date _____

*Source:*  UNITE HERE Web site: www.unitehere.org/resources/docs/DiscGrievFactSheet6-10-02.doc

**Figure 4.3** A sample Discipline Grievance Fact Sheet used by a union. The same points may be adapted for a retail company manager's fair and thorough investigation of a grievance situation, to help determine whether a disciplinary action by the company was handled correctly.

**there can be one.** Instead, tell the worker advocate what you'll do next, and when. Whether it is issuing a decision yourself or taking the grievance up the chain of command, always keep the worker advocate in the loop. This will minimize misunderstandings, show respect to the worker advocate, and allow the worker advocate to keep the grievant informed—all of which contribute to minimizing employee-employer conflict and maximizing workplace productivity.[13]

Remember, the overall goal of a grievance investigation is to get it settled, without lingering ill feelings on the part of any party to the complaint. Grievances are like any other type of disagreement—some uncover an error in judgment on the part of the employee; others point out a problem with overzealous management, or with an unfair company policy that truly does need to be addressed. The cooperation skills stressed in Chapter 3 may come in handy for managers who are wrestling with a tough situation based on a union grievance.

## CHAPTER SUMMARY

The retail industry is not highly unionized, although some store chains, and some parts of the country, have more labor union members than others. Managers may also deal with people in ancillary professions—warehouse employees, transportation workers, employees of suppliers, and so on—who are unionized. It is always smart to be informed about their agreements with your company and the terms of the union contracts.

This chapter introduced the names and goals of the largest unions in the United States that are involved with the retail trade. It also explained the basics about how the national and local unions are organized, the differences between craft and industrial unions, and what shop stewards and business agents do.

The ideal union contract benefits both the employees and the company for which they work. It spells out the pay, benefits, and working conditions of the employees, and it outlines the terms for a company to benefit from the union's highly skilled workforce. The business world being what it is, however, not everything goes according to contract. This is why most contracts also stipulate a policy for grievances, which are employee complaints about the employer that are most often (but not always) related to specific terms of the contract. The chapter ended with a step-by-step process that managers can use to investigate a grievance.

## DISCUSSION QUESTIONS

1. What kinds of protection does a union offer its worker members?
2. What is the difference between a craft union and an industrial union?
3. Why is it important for a retail department manager and/or store owner to know how a union is generally structured?
4. What kinds of things do you think would prompt a grievance based on an employer's past practices? Would nonunion employees have the same gripe about these issues as union employees—but less power to resolve them?
5. Knowing what you now know about unions, what would you suggest that a union and a company might do to ensure a better relationship? Write a paragraph on behalf of each party.

## ENDNOTES

1. Barry T. Hirsh and David A. Macpherson, "Union Membership and Coverage Database from the Current Population Survey," *Industrial & Labor Relations Review*, Volume 56, No. 2, January 2003.
2. *This Is the AFL-CIO*, www.aflcio.org, Web site of the AFL-CIO, Washington, D.C., February 2005.
3. *A Brief History of Unions*, www.uswa.org, Web site of the United Steel Workers of America, Pittsburgh, Pennsylvania, February 2005.
4. See endnote 2.
5. *What Is Unite Here?*, www.unitehere.org, Web site of UNITE HERE, New York, February 2005.
6. *International Ladies Garment Workers Union*, The Eleanor Roosevelt Papers, Eleanor Roosevelt National Historic Site, Hyde Park, New York, 2003.
7. *Where We Stand*, Web site of Industrial Workers of the World, www.iww.org, Philadelphia, Pennsylvania, February 2005.
8. *Teamster Facts and Demographics*, Web site of the International Brotherhood of Teamsters, www.teamster.org, Washington, D.C., February 2005.
9. Excerpt from mission statement, AFL-CIO, Washington, D.C.
10. *How the AFL-CIO Works*, Web site of AFL-CIO, Washington, D.C.
11. Definitions from Industrial Workers of the World, Philadelphia, Pennsylvania.

12. Grievance descriptions from IBEW Local 1613, Kansas City, Missouri, on Web site http://home.earthlink.net/~local1613.grievance_description.html, February 2005.

13. *How to Investigate a Grievance*, www.unitehere.org, on Web site of UNITE HERE, New York.

# 5

---

# EMPLOYEE
# BENEFITS

---

The slang term for benefits is "perks." It's short for *perquisites*, a word for something added to regular profit or pay, especially something that is customary or expected. Indeed, employee benefits are expected by today's workforce. In negotiations with prospective employees, perks are often just as important as wages—and, as you'll learn in this chapter, even more so for some job candidates.

Of course, benefits are also among most employers' major expenses. So careful attention must be paid to employee benefit packages at all levels to enhance their upsides and minimize their downsides.

Unless they work in the human resource department, most managers do not design or even offer advice on the benefit packages offered by their companies. They simply work with and monitor existing plans—not only as managers, but as recipients of the benefits, too. A manager's key benefits-related function, however, is to make sure the company's benefits package is properly understood by its workers, and that promised benefits are dispensed appropriately and in a timely manner.

This chapter explains some of the most common compensation package and workplace benefits, including these topics:

- Mandatory, voluntary, and individual benefits
- Employees' expectations about benefits
- General compensation trends and costs
- Benefit package types and trends
- Health care coverage and costs
- Other compensation forms, including nonfinancial and flexible benefits

Employee benefits fall into two major categories: as part of a compensation package or as part of the workplace environment. **Compensation benefits** have a financial value that may be easily calculated. Examples of compensation benefits include

| | |
|---|---|
| Health insurance | Paid vacation time |
| Use of company vehicle | Vision and dental insurance |
| Paid sick leave | Stock options and/or |
| Child care | Parental leave |
| Elder care | Workers' compensation or other |
| 401(k) retirement plan or | disability insurance |
| pension plan | Discounts on merchandise or services |

Workplace benefits are nice "extras" that make working at a certain company a bit more convenient or personable. They are often lifestyle-related. Examples of **workplace benefits** include

| | | |
|---|---|---|
| Flextime | Cafeterias or break rooms | Reserved parking |
| Job sharing | Free coffee and donuts | Protected parking |
| Shower rooms | Workout rooms or gym | Employee-of-the- |
| Financial planning | memberships | month parking |
| services | | |

Monitoring the benefits program is a continuing process for managers at all levels. For senior management, it starts with designing the benefits offerings, individually and as "packages." For all managers, these become an integral part of the hiring package, as well as a point of negotiation in the following situations:

- Claims are made.
- Contracts, salary reviews, and promotions come up.
- Employees quit, are terminated, are injured, or die.
- Employees retire after pension-qualifying terms of service.

In most cases, workplaces are also required to post standard notices to advise employees of the existence of some state and federal benefits (such as minimum wages and workers' compensation insurance), and their rights, ability to file claims, and the like. It's generally up to managers to ensure these notices are posted and are changed as new information or compliance rules are added.

## A BIT OF BENEFITS BACKGROUND

Most Americans get their retirement and health insurance coverage from job-based benefits, either through their own employment or that of a family member. Generally, benefits are a combination of individual, business, and government contributions of various types, and they fall into the following three categories:

**Mandatory benefits.** Workers' compensation, family and medical leave, unemployment insurance, and Social Security are mandatory benefits under federal and/or state law. Companies and, in most cases, workers must contribute part of their earnings to finance these programs.

**Voluntary benefits.** Most retirement plans and health insurance are provided by businesses to workers on a voluntary basis. The government, however, usually encourages voluntary employee benefits through various tax incentives, to both the workers who receive them and the companies that provide them.

**Individual programs.** Individual retirement plans and other financial security programs—such as life insurance and death benefits—are also encouraged by government through favorable tax rates and other tax-based incentives.[1]

Compensation benefits have grown in size and scope during the last several decades primarily because they are a win-win proposition for both companies and the workers they hire. If unions are involved, another "win" can be added to the proposition.

*For companies*, benefit packages are a way to help ensure worker loyalty, beyond simply paying higher wages. When workers can accrue better pensions and longer vacations through job longevity, they tend to stay longer, thus creating lower worker turnover, In turn, this reduces company recruiting, hiring, and training costs. Companies also save money because their ability to buy at group rates means they can provide workers with benefits for a fraction of the equivalent wages they'd have to pay to enable the workers to buy the comparable benefits individually on the open market.

*For workers*, benefit packages tend to increase nontaxable compensation, giving them necessary benefits like insurance without having to pay income taxes on these benefits. Employees pay less for the benefits because of group rates as well. And for lower-paid or less senior workers, benefits packages tend to equalize compensation in ways that are helpful to the lower-paid workers without aggravating those with more seniority or higher-paid skill sets.

*For unions*, benefit packages are a great way for them to make deals for their members without costing the company too much, and getting proportionately more for their lowest-paid members, all of which makes the unions and their leaders look good.

## Employees' Expectations

Now let's turn our attention for a moment to the people the benefits are designed to, in a word, benefit! Human resource professionals point to the fact that today's employers are, for the most part, dealing with three different generations of workers—and each group expects different things from their workplace.

The Baby Boomers (born between 1945 and 1965) are now in their 40s, 50s and 60s, and they're the most loyal of the employee groups. They've made it to management positions, and many say they'd rather keep working and stay active than retire at age 65. They know the value of their years of work experience, and they expect excellent benefits that will increase as they age. For these workers, the importance of benefits often even outweighs the hourly or monthly salary.

Younger workers, members of Generations X and Y, are far more salary-driven. They have grown up seeing many companies reduce benefits and break promises to workers—including their parents—so they are very independent, and not especially loyal as employees. Gen Xers (born between 1965 and 1980) are now young parents. They are concerned about work/life balance, child care issues, and career development. Their

Generation Y counterparts (born between 1980 and 1994) are even more technologically competent, and just as independent as the Gen Xers. If they don't feel they're being paid well or treated well, they'll move on. They are interested in personal career development, and they'd rather have higher wages than great benefits. The benefits they *do* have, they want to manage themselves.

Michael Maciekowich, national director of the New York–based human resource consulting firm Astron Solutions, says flexibility in benefit offerings is the only way to satisfy this multigenerational workforce. For instance, he suggests companies use seniority as a factor in paying for health care coverage—the longer a person works at the company, the greater amount the company pays. And for younger employees, giving salary increases even when business is down is the way to keep them happy.

"I always tell my clients when they're having a bad year: 'If there was ever a time to pay your stars more, now's the time,'" explains Maciekowich. "Talk about creating loyalty from them!"[2]

Whether you agree or not with the characterizations of the employee groups mentioned here, the fact is that your workers' needs when it comes to savings, insurance, and even time off will vary depending on their ages, lifestyles, and other highly individual personal priorities. Employers cannot be everything to everyone, but benefits designed for maximum flexibility can adapt the best to meet a variety of individual situations.

## What Companies Pay for Benefits

Compensation benefits as a percentage of total payroll costs have varied during the past decade, from a 1994 high of 29.2 percent to a 2001 low of 27.4 percent of payroll in 2000 and 2001. (See Figure 5-1.)

According to Bureau of Labor (BLS) statistics, total employee compensation costs in 2002 (the most current year for which figures are available at this writing) were $22.14 per labor hour, up from $13.42 in 1987. This represents an average annual increase of 3.4 percent.

During the same time period (1987 to 2002), the cost of benefits to U.S. companies rose from 26.8 percent of total compensation costs, to 27.4 percent of total compensation costs.

Starting in 1996, BLS began tracking private-sector costs for Social Security and Medicare. Social Security cost employers $0.84 per labor hour then, and rose to $1.08 in 2002. Employer Medicare costs were $0.21 per labor hour in 1996 and increased to $0.26 in 2002.

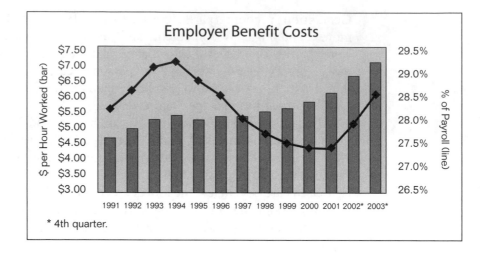

**Figure 5-1**
Employer benefit costs. (Source: Bureau of Labor Statistics, Washington, D.C.)

Please note that these are general figures—they do not reflect cost variations due to company size, the type of business or occupation, full- versus part-time workers, union status, and the state in which the company is located. Larger businesses and organizations, for example, usually have higher total compensation costs. Companies with more than 500 employees averaged $30.29 per labor hour in 2002, compared with $18.87 per labor hour for companies with fewer than 100 employees.

Other insightful comparisons of benefit costs include

- Manufacturing industries ($25.88 per labor hour) versus service industries ($21.11)
- White-collar occupations ($26.77 per labor hour) versus blue-collar occupations ($20.68) and service occupations ($11.25)
- Full-time workers ($22.14 per labor hour) versus part-time workers ($12.30)
- Union workers ($30.29 per labor hour) versus nonunion workers ($21.16)[3]

## Benefit Types and Trends

Most full-time workers in the United States today enjoy some form of sick leave, paid vacations, and company-subsidized health insurance. Almost 60 percent of full-time U.S. workers also have employment-based retirement plans.

Eighty-three percent of union workers are covered by retirement plans, as are 70 percent of all workers who earn more than $15 per hour. Sixty-five percent of workers in companies with more than 100 employees have some form of company-sponsored retirement plan.[4]

There are two primary types of benefits packages for workers covered by retirement plans: defined benefit plans and defined contribution packages. A **defined benefit plan** (DB) is the traditional pension plan: a specified benefit amount and duration financed entirely by employer contributions according to employee longevity and earnings formulas. A **defined contribution package** (DC) plan, on the other hand, is generally paid out as an annuity and not transferable from job to job. DC plans do not specify benefit amounts or duration and are usually financed with both company and worker contributions. With DC plans, workers can make several choices about how these contributions are invested, giving them more control and responsibility over the ultimate value of the fund. DC plans are also transferable; the worker's accrued benefits can be rolled over from one job to the next.

As shown in Figure 5-2, the number of DB plans has declined significantly during the past 30 years. This is partly a consequence of workers who have more career changes today than in past generations and seldom stay with one company for their whole career, and partly because smaller companies have converted their DB plans to DC plans—like 401(k)s—or ended pension plans entirely. On the other hand, because they make sense for companies and workers alike, the number of DC plans has increased significantly during the past few decades (also as seen in Figure 5-2). DC plans allow companies to avoid the cost and uncertainty of open-ended pension commitments, and they allow workers

**Figure 5-2** An increasing number of companies are choosing DC plans instead of DB plans, partly because employees are less likely to remain at one company throughout their career. (Source: The Employee Benefit Research Institute, Education and Research Fund, Washington, D.C., December 2004. All rights reserved.)

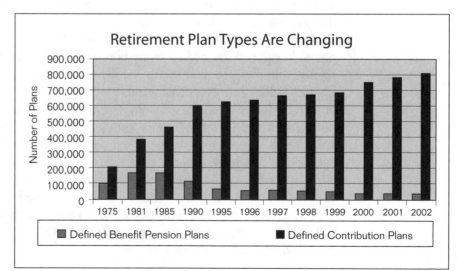

to keep the retirement benefits they've accrued at one company when they go on to the next.

Perhaps the most commonly used DC plan is the "401(k)," named for the plan outlined in Section 401(k) of the Internal Revenue Code, signed into law in 1978.

Section 401(k) authorizes employers to voluntarily make pretax contributions to an employee savings plans, and to automatically deduct an employee-specified amount from the worker's pretax paycheck. Unlike normal savings plans, 401(k) assets are not taxed as long as they remain in the account, but there is a penalty for withdrawing the funds before age 59 1/2.

Companies of all types can establish 401(k) plans, and they are authorized within certain guidelines to impose a variety of eligibility requirements and restrictions for employee participation. Your company policies may include provisions for time in service, union membership, U.S. citizenship, full-time/part-time status, and so on as prerequisites for (or restrictions on) 401(k) participation.[5]

## Other Benefit Packages

**Cash balance plans** are a combination of DB and DC package elements designed to give companies a tighter handle on future pension commitments. With a cash balance plan, the company usually contributes a defined amount each year, based on worker income and seniority, and guarantees the account will grow annually by a fixed percentage. When workers reach retirement age, they generally have the option of taking the final amount, either as an annuity or a lump sum.

Some employers in the past converted DB plans into cash balance plans, but this prompted so many lawsuits and so much regulatory ambiguity that most companies now shy away from such conversions.[6]

**Individual retirement accounts** (IRAs) allow workers to individually invest in a retirement account. Contributions aren't tax-deductible, but withdrawals are tax-free as long as the account has been in existence for five years and the worker does not make withdrawals before age 59 1/2. Recently, Congress authorized the creation of nonretirement IRAs for educational and other purposes, and IRAs have long been used as a temporary depository for 401(k) money transferred (or "rolled over") from one company's plan to another to avoid the 20 percent "withholding"—the penalty paid to the IRS when money is prematurely withdrawn.[7]

A **Keogh account** is a personal retirement account for a self-employed person, a tax-deferred investment account that allows the worker to deposit tax-free money into personal retirement accounts. Keoghs may also be used by employers (often small-business owners) to set up retirement plans for their workers.

Like IRAs and 401(k) plans, Keogh plans have a yearly contribution limit; unlike those plans, which are limited to $2,000 and $15,000 respectively, self-employed workers can save up to 20 percent or $30,000 per year—whichever is greater—of their annual net self-employment income.[8]

## HEALTH CARE COVERAGE AND COSTS

Health care benefits are the largest and fastest-growing corporate expenses today, outpacing by far the money that corporations contribute to employee retirement plans. It is standard for company-provided or company-subsidized health care packages to include medical, hospital, and surgical coverage, and prescription drug benefits. Many companies have further expanded their health care coverage—and of course, their costs—to include vision and dental benefits, pregnancy benefits, substance abuse and psychiatric treatment, and a variety of wellness and/or physical fitness programs. Some employers have added several types of elder care to their packages.

The biggest problem in the health care field is that health insurance premiums, even at the "package" level offered by employers with group rates, are increasing much faster than inflation. Higher premiums, along with rising costs due to expanded coverage, have led to a variety of legislative actions to rein them in—including universal and/or guaranteed health care proposals, and other programs that impose a number of additional burdens on business. Debate continues about these potential legislative solutions, and about the kind of private sector-government mix that will actually result in a viable program that delivers good health care without bankrupting either businesses or the government.

At the same time, unionized companies face increasing pressure to extend health care benefits to their retirees, and many are responding to this pressure by increasing the proportion of health care costs borne by their retirees. Active employees are not immune to this trend—companies that used to cover health insurance costs in full have begun to require

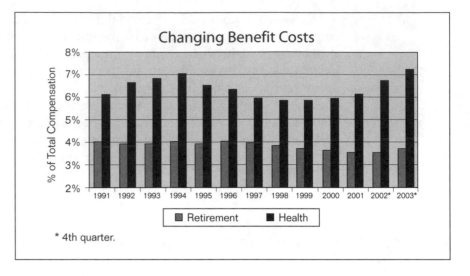

**Figure 5-3** Heath and retirement benefits are voluntary and not all companies provide them; so the true costs of these benefits for the companies that do provide them are higher than the numbers reflected in these aggregate figures.

contributions from employees; those that shared the cost with employees are making the employees pay a greater share.

Another cost-saving measure used by companies is moving away from free-choice health plans to restricted-choice health maintenance organizations (HMOs) and physicians' networks, and imposing a variety of restrictions and/or conditions on surgery and certain other forms of care.

Many companies are also trying to save money by finding ways to exclude certain of their workers from eligibility for company-provided health care, usually by restricting coverage to full-time employees or workers who have a defined amount of seniority. A growing number of companies are also reducing their employee benefit costs by moving away from permanent full- and part-time employees, and outsourcing some jobs to contract workers or "temps," who may command somewhat higher wages but receive no benefits at all.

Finally, for many smaller companies, providing any kind of health coverage for their workers is simply not an option—it's too expensive. The National Association for the Self-Employed (NASE) estimates that employees of so-called microbusinesses—those with fewer than 10 employees, including many small retailers—pay 18 percent more for health insurance than their counterparts in companies with over 200 employees. NASE says of the 45 million people in the United States without health insurance, 60 percent of them are workers (or their dependents) in small businesses.[9]

# GUARANTEED INCOME PLANS

Job security and income maintenance are not parts of a benefit package per se, but they are a significant part of overall employee costs per labor hour. There are several established programs through which workers can keep the money coming in even if their jobs have ended, they've been discharged, or they were injured in the workplace—which, in the minds of most employees, will certainly qualify as "benefits."

**Unemployment compensation** is one of the oldest and best-known income maintenance programs. Employers and the U.S. government contribute to a fund that provides up to 26 weeks of checks based on the amount of money a worker has earned during a prescribed period prior to leaving his or her job, which the worker can apply for and receive while they actively search for a new job.

**Workers' compensation** is a type of insurance, a well-established program funded by company and government contributions for employees who can't work after being injured on the job. Most policies also cover diseases "caused or aggravated by the conditions of employment."[10] Workers' comp policies are administered by each state's insurance commission; there are also federal workers' comp programs for federal employees.

**Disability insurance** is another way for workers to maintain an income in the event of either workplace or nonworkplace injuries that make them (at least temporarily) unemployable. Unlike unemployment and workers' compensation, the worker almost always pays for disability insurance premiums.

There are a couple of other programs that are extremely rare in retail businesses but should be mentioned nonetheless because they may apply to certain unionized employees:

**Supplemental Unemployment Benefits (SUBs)** are income maintenance plans first created by the United Auto Workers in its 1955 contract. They still exist today in industries with boom-bust cycles prone to big, headline-generating layoffs and other forms of job loss. SUB benefits are meant to enhance and prolong standard unemployment and workers' compensation benefits by providing up to 95 percent of a worker's regular income for up to nine months.

**Guaranteed Income Stream Benefits (GIS)** programs pick up where SUBs leave off. They provide a guaranteed income until retirement for very senior workers in industries where there is long-term "structural" unemployment: plant closings, large-scale layoffs, and various types of permanent job losses. This benefit was created in 1982 by the UAW to address structural unemployment in the auto industry. GIS plans are longer term in nature than SUB; they provide up to 75 percent of a worker's regular income for several years, but they also include 45 provisions that encourage both workers and management to find new jobs in different industries for laid-off or displaced workers.

## OTHER TYPES OF BENEFITS

Companies offer a variety of other benefits to workers, beyond the standard benefit packages. Some are mandatory by federal law—such as overtime pay and maternity/paternity leave—but others are purely voluntary and differ not only between industries but between companies within industries as well. These benefits fall into four major categories: supplemental pay, leave programs, personal services benefits, and family-based benefits.

### Supplemental Pay

**Overtime** or premium pay is the primary form of supplemental pay and is required by the Fair Labor Standards Act (FLSA) and most states for any workers on the job for more than 40 hours per week. The FLSA requires overtime to be at least 50 percent higher than the normal wage rate ("time and a half"), and various companies, unions, and states often set the rate at double the usual wage for holidays and/or workdays that exceed 10 to 12 hours.

**Shift differentials** are another form of supplemental pay, usually awarded to evening and night shift workers in companies that operate 24 hours a day or, at least, more than "regular business hours." Generally, the overnight or "graveyard" shift workers receive the highest shift differential, and evening or "swing" shift workers receive a lower shift differential. Day shift workers are usually not eligible for shift differential pay.

**Bonuses** are also considered as supplemental pay—but only if they are not tied to production or sales goals. Examples include contract-signing bonuses, year-end bonuses, Christmas or other holiday bonuses, and lump-sum payments made in lieu of pay increases.

**Profit-sharing plans** were granted only to managers and company officers until recently, but now they have become a more common worker benefit as companies offer them in exchange for wage and pension concessions, or to increase worker loyalty. Profit-sharing plans generally activate when company profits reach a designated level; profits are then issued as either cash or company stock. Profit sharing is expected to become even more common in the future because it rewards workers for more or better product or service output, and because it is one way to keep employees focused on quality control and profitability.

## Leave Programs

As with supplemental pay, most companies offer paid time off to workers for a variety of situations. Some of these "leave programs" are mandated by federal, state, or local law, while others are provided as part of a union contract or solely at the discretion of an individual manager or company. If you're a manager, be sure you know and understand your company's policy about leave.

**Paid holidays and vacations** are the oldest and most traditional types of paid-leave programs, and in most cases, they apply to all workers regardless of seniority. Holiday observances vary from company to company, and from private sector to public sector, but public-sector firms usually observe far more holidays. Many companies allow only the six "major" paid holidays per year—New Year's Day, Memorial Day, Independence Day, Labor Day, Thanksgiving, and Christmas—but in retail, holidays take on a whole new meaning, since they are often busier than in other industries. President's Day, Valentine's Day, and the entire weekend after Thanksgiving, for example, are traditionally big sale days, and work schedules must be made accordingly.

Some companies also provide so-called personal days or "floating" holidays that employees can take (with advance notice and approval) for birthdays, anniversaries, or unspecified reasons.

Paid vacations are a leave benefit generally tied to worker seniority or time in service. Most companies require at least one year of service to be eligible for paid vacation, and initial vacation eligibility tends to be one or two weeks in length. In most companies, this figure increases to two or three weeks after five years, and customarily grows to four weeks for workers with 20 years of service with a given company. Retail firms are no exception.

**Sick leave** is also a common paid benefit, and most companies realize its value. The idea behind paid sick leave is more practical than empathic—it reduces the chances of people who are ill coming to work infecting others. Standard sick leave varies in number of days from company to company, but it tends to be allotted in full-day or half-day increments for each month or year worked. Some companies also allow workers to "cash in" unused sick leave, while others do not, creating a reverse incentive to "call in sick" in order to make use of the benefit. Other companies allow employees to use their sick leave to tend to sick family members, notably children, as well as for themselves.

**Leave banks** are a growing trend in the way companies deal with worker leave. In a "leave bank," all of a worker's paid time off is consolidated into a single account, and the worker can draw on it as needed.

## Personal Services Benefits

Companies have long offered benefits like life insurance and various forms of physical fitness or "wellness" programs for their employees, but personal services benefits have expanded during the last decade to include legal services, financial advice, and different types of elder care.

**Life insurance** is the most common personal service benefit, but as with most benefits, it has expanded significantly in recent years. In past decades, workers could get annual term life policies through their employer that covered only death and, in some cases, dismemberment or severe disability. Today, many workers enjoy access to insurance coverage once reserved for top management—universal life insurance plans with death benefits and a savings component that allows workers to invest a portion of their premium in an account or an annuity with a predetermined rate of return.

**Wellness or fitness programs** are designed to encourage healthy lifestyles that, in turn, should result in a more productive workforce. Examples include on-site fitness centers and/or off-site gym memberships, aerobic and other types of fitness classes, nutrition and weight control education, and a variety of health evaluations, appraisals, and monitoring.

**Legal services** are another growing part of employee benefits, especially as the cost of independently paying for attorneys goes up. These perks are generally paid for (in full or part) by the employee. Some companies ask employees to pay a nominal monthly fee that entitles them to a certain amount of basic service: drafting wills; reviewing deeds, leases, and other legal documents; writing legal letters; and providing consultations, either in person or by phone. Mediation or arbitration and more complex legal matters may be resolved under separate contract with individual employees.

## Family-based Benefits

Two-income households and single-parent families have become the new norms in most American workplaces—but remember, the Family and Medical Leave Act discussed in Chapter 2 does not apply to companies with fewer than 50 employees. All of this has sparked an ever-growing need for family-based benefits that include health care for all family members, sick leave to care for ailing children or elderly family members, maternity and paternity leave, and flexible work schedules.

**Child care** is the most widely needed family-based benefit, but the majority of companies still leave child care issues and costs to be dealt with by each worker. A few companies offer company-based day care for their workers, or financial assistance for this purpose; even more provide information, child care referrals, and other support.

A look at *Working Mother* magazine's annual list of "The 100 Best Companies for Working Mothers" should give any retail manager ideas for how to improve company child care benefits. Minneapolis-based Target Corporation was on the list in 2004, for a family-friendly benefits lineup that includes

- 16-weeks of job-guaranteed maternity leave
- Full pay for six weeks of maternity leave for salaried employees
- 70 percent pay for six weeks of maternity leave for hourly employees
- Emergency backup child care agreements with two national day care chains
- 10 days off per year to deal with sick children or care for elders[11]

Some unions have actively pursued day care as a company-provided benefit for their members. Among the more notable was the Communications Workers of America/International Brotherhood of Electrical Workers (CWA/IBEW) contracts in 1989 and 1992 with AT&T. Those contracts required the company to set aside $5 million and $7.5 million, respectively, to either assist workers with finding day care or to establish company-run day care centers.[12] Other unions have taken it upon themselves to create union-supported day care centers as a member benefit.

**Elder care** programs take several forms, from home health aides and nursing services (with premiums paid for by employees) to company-based support systems that offer counseling, consultations, workshops, seminars, and flexible scheduling for employees with dependent senior citizens in their care. Only about one-fourth of U.S. companies currently offer elder care benefits, but 15 percent of workers are juggling at least some of the care and support for an elderly relative, a number that is expected to grow in coming decades with the overall aging of the U.S. population. A Society of Human Resource Management's 2003 Elder Care Survey indicated almost half of HR professionals reported an increase in the number of employees who are dealing with issues such as these:

- Missing a full day of work (59 percent)
- Encountering workday interruptions (44 percent)
- Experiencing stress-related health problems (29 percent)

Further, 16 percent of the survey respondents said their companies had experienced either attrition or turnover due to workers' competing elder care demands.[13]

**Maternity and paternity benefits** are now mandatory—but only for companies with more than 50 employees—as part of the Family and Medical Leave Act. They are required to provide up to 12 weeks of unpaid, job-protected leave for eligible employees due to the adoption or birth of a child, or the serious illness of the employee, or the employee's spouse, child, or parent. It also requires the company to maintain health care benefits during the leave period, if those benefits were part of the employee's basic compensation package. Some unions have tried during contract bargaining to make family leave a paid benefit and to extend the leave duration to as much as a year.

When an employee knows and can plan for the leave, he or she must give 30 days' notice before taking it, although there are a number of exemptions—several of which may apply either to part-time or seasonal employees or to managers:

- Employees who have worked less than 24 hours per week during the preceding year, or who have worked for the company less than one year
- Teachers or other instructors during the school year
- Employees whose salaries or wages fall within the top 10 percent of the company's employees
- Employees whose spouses work at the same company (they can take a total of 12 weeks between them)

## BUILDING IN MAXIMUM FLEXIBILITY

Flexible workdays, or **flextime**, is another benefit that is growing in popularity with retailers and their employees because of its win-win nature. Workers benefit by being better able to take care of children, senior citizens, or personal business. Companies benefit because this flexibility generally results in happier and more productive workers. Flextime, staggered work hours, and even some types of telecommuting may also allow employees in heavily congested urban areas the chance to reduce commute times and avoid the aggravation created by rush hour traffic.

Flextime also includes compressed work schedules (more hours per day, but fewer days per week on the job) and job sharing (when two or more employees "share" hours to create a single, full-time work presence). Retailers, both large and small, have a few distinct advantages over other types of businesses when it comes to these types of benefits, as the nature of retail scheduling lends itself well to part-time and flexible work arrangements.

All these changes in traditional work schedules and job structures are primarily worker-based; managers and even unions resisted these benefits at first because managers feared workers would be less productive and unions feared workers might be exploited. However, the employees appreciated the convenience afforded by flextime. In most cases, they have made it work not just for themselves but for their employers' bottom lines as well.

## Flexible Benefit Plans

Flexibility may be built into the benefits plans themselves, as a common-sense response to the growing number of two-income families where dual incomes result in duplicate benefits, as well as a nod to childless workers who get short shrift in many companies simply because they don't have the scheduling problems associated with parenting. With a flexible benefit plan, each employee receives a dollar amount to be used on benefits and can allocate it as he or she sees fit.

There are two major types of flexible benefit plans:

**Cafeteria plans** are similar to the "leave banks" described earlier in this chapter. The company assigns a dollar amount to the total benefits allotted to each worker, and provides a list of benefits from which workers can draw based on their own needs.

**Reimbursement accounts** allow pretax income to be used for various health and family-based benefits.

Flexible benefits are especially useful when both workers in a family have health insurance coverage. One worker's health care plan can cover the family, while the other is "traded" in a cafeteria plan for other benefits. They are also a way for employers to hold down costs by negotiating lump-sum dollar amounts for benefits and their inflation- or premium-based increases, instead of embarking on more complicated (and usually more expensive) renegotiations for copayments, deductibles, and total coverage.

There are drawbacks to flexible benefit plans, however. They can be difficult for management to track—which employee has signed up for which benefits? Who's using them and who is not? How often are changes allowed, and increases or adjustments made? How are workers kept fully informed about their options?

Also, there are potential cost increases for some of the less popular benefits that not very many workers "choose" from the list. This ultimately impacts the group pricing for those benefits.

## CHAPTER SUMMARY

Benefits come in two basic forms: either a compensation benefit that has a specific cost or financial value, like health insurance or matching a worker's retirement plan contributions, or a lifestyle-related perk, such as an on-site fitness facility or coffee and donuts with Friday paychecks.

Most companies offer some of both, and the mix often depends on the needs of the workforce, reflected (at least in part) on their ages and expectations. The typical U.S. employee today receives at least some sick leave, paid vacation time, and paid holidays. Medical insurance benefits are a requirement for many, although in small companies, they have become too expensive to maintain.

This chapter covered the ways in which compensation plans have changed over the last few decades to reflect changes in workforce demographics as well as the economy. There are now more defined contribution plans (DC) than defined benefits (DB) plans, since DC plans can follow an employee to a new job. With fewer workers spending entire careers at one company, this is an important change. Other changes include companies cutting back on fast-rising benefit costs like health insurance by offering more limited coverage, making retirees and current employees pay a greater percentage of their health insurance costs, or contracting with HMOs to provide health care.

Benefits designed for job security and income maintenance in case of accidents or injuries, layoffs, or unexpected job losses are mandated by the federal government in some cases. Companies must pay unemployment compensation and workers' compensation into funds that are administered by government agencies.

Flexibility is extremely important to today's workforce, many of whom are caring for children and/or elderly relatives. Companies may provide a cafeteria-style plan, in which each employee receives points or dollars in an account and can choose to spend them on any of the company's benefit offerings. Flextime is also considered a benefit—the option to job-share, work slightly different hours than the norm, or organize a less traditional workweek to fit other priorities into a busy life.

## DISCUSSION QUESTIONS

1. In the list of "insightful comparisons" early in this chapter, what do the benefits costs of various types of workers say about the value of different types of work in our culture?
2. Which do you think are more important to entry-level workers in the retail industry: compensation benefits or workplace benefits? Why?
3. Select another country and research the average wages and types of benefits workers receive there. Compare and contrast retail jobs in both countries if you can find the information to do so. Write a short report to share with the class.
4. What forms do supplemental pay benefits take, and why are they important?
5. What kinds of advantages and disadvantages do you think the retail industry has when it comes to offering the various perks in this chapter to its workforce?

## ENDNOTES

1. ©The Employee Benefit Research Institute, Education and Research Fund, Washington, D.C., December 2004. All rights reserved.
2. ©Astron Solutions, LLC, New York, 2005.
3. See endnote 1.
4. See endnote 1.
5. "What is a 401k Plan? Here Is a Quick Overview," Web site of 401khelpcenter.com, LLP, Portland, Oregon.
6. See Endnote 1.
7. "What is a Roth IRA?", Web site of Atlantic Financial, Inc., Norwell, Massachusetts.
8. "What is a Keogh?", Glossary of *BusinessWeek Online* magazine, The McGraw-Hill Companies, Inc., New York, 2005.
9. Statistics from the National Association for the Self-Employed, North Richland Hills, Texas, March 2005.

10. *Workers Compensation and Employers Liability Insurance Policy,* National Council on Compensation Insurance, NCII Holdings, Inc., Boca Raton, Florida, 1992.

11. "100 Best Companies for Working Mothers 2004," *Working Mother,* New York, 2004.

12. Howard Hayghe, "Employers and Child Care: What Roles Do They Play?" *Monthly Labor Review,* September 1998.

13. *SHRM Elder Care Survey,* Society for Human Resource Management, Alexandria, Virginia, 2003.

# 6

# RETENTION AND MOTIVATION

You've hired a workforce, and you understand the basic employment laws and benefit plans. But even the companies that do everything "right" are concerned about the issue of employee retention—and retail companies more so than others. U.S. Bureau of Labor statistics for 2004 indicate that turnover rates average just over 33 percent in retail jobs. That means every year, one out of every three retail employees leaves their job. People who voluntarily quit (usually to take a new job elsewhere) make up 30.2 percent of the total; another 3 percent choose to retire.[1] There are even scarier figures elsewhere in this chapter about retail employees' myriad workplace frustrations. So in this chapter, we focus on how to keep good employees, including the following topics:

- The impact of employee turnover
- Retention as a process or system
- Working with employees' feelings as well as facts
- Why workers stay, and why they leave
- Dealing with change
- Creating supportive systems
- Conducting effective exit interviews

In industry overall, the average employee turnover today is 3.5 years. In short, no sooner does a person become truly familiar with a job and a company than he or she is gone again. This can be especially frustrating for managers, who count on those well-trained, trusted employees to keep systems running smoothly, from floor sales to retail buying to back-office functions. Let's do what we can to prevent it in *your* company.

## THE CASE FOR EMPLOYEE RETENTION

The sheer volume of workers in the "revolving doors" of retail is alarming, and it points to the need for managers to make employee retention and satisfaction a greater priority for several reasons—not the least of which is the cost associated with hiring new workers. It costs an average of one-fourth of an employee's annual pay to hire a replacement when that worker leaves. This includes payment of any benefits or bonuses owed the outgoing worker at the time of departure, advertising and/or recruiting activities to find new job candidates, the interviewing and screening processes, and training the new person. Even for an entry-level job, these costs can add up to more than $6,000 per person.[2]

There are also indirect costs, including the loss of the person's skills, knowledge, and experience. If the worker goes "across town" to a competitor with a better offer, the impact can be even worse long term.

It is true that not all turnovers are bad, and not every employee who gives a two-week notice to leave will be sorely missed. Sometimes, it's best for everyone when a poor performer or a person with an attitude problem decides to go elsewhere. But if that is not the case, resignations

Percent of Employees

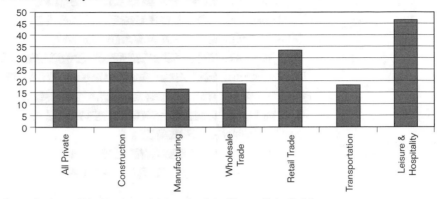

**Figure 6-1**
Employment Turnover
by Industry. Voluntary
Quits and Retirements
Replaced by New
Hires. Percent of
Workforce by
Industry, Annual Rate,
August 2004.

*Source:* Employment Policy Foundation tabulation and analysis of Bureau of Labor Statistics,
Job Openings and Labor Turnover Survey data.

can create a morale factor that may be difficult to quantify. The remaining employees in a department or on a team may understandably resent having to pick up the increased workload until a new person is hired. If the department has experienced frequent departures, the workers who are left may be feeling nervous—should I be looking for a new job, too? Am I missing out on something better by staying here? Managers should look for these signs of discontent after each departure.

Better yet, they should be aware of the clues long before a resignation takes place. In the remainder of this chapter, we'll discuss how to make people feel welcome and supported from their first experience with your company, how to recognize when they are wrestling with their own discontent, and what, if anything, you can do about it as a manager.

Percent of Employees

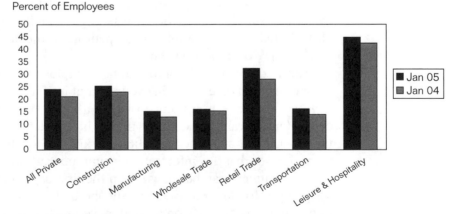

**Figure 6-2**
Voluntary Quits by
Industry. Percent
of Employees by
Industry.

*Source:* Employment Policy Foundation tabulation and analysis of Bureau of Labor Statistics,
Job Openings and Labor Turnover Survey data.

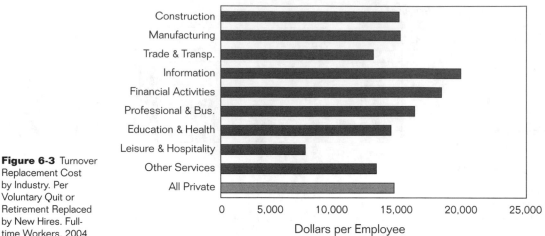

**Figure 6-3** Turnover Replacement Cost by Industry. Per Voluntary Quit or Retirement Replaced by New Hires. Full-time Workers, 2004 Four-quarter Average.

*Source:* Employment Policy Foundation tabulation and analysis of Bureau of Labor Statistics, Employer Cost of Employee Compensation data.

## Retention as a Process

All too often, organizations and their managers see a series of human resources tasks before them—interview, hire, train, review performance, discipline, transfer, and/or promote as necessary, and so on. What they fail to see is that these tasks are all pieces of a total process or system, with the end result of developing a loyal and efficient employee.

The process begins with the recruitment and interviewing of job candidates, discussed in greater detail in Chapter 1. If the advertisement and interviewer have provided a realistic assessment of the job and required skills, if the candidate is a good fit for the responsibilities and truly understands what he or she is taking on, and if the salary and benefits offered are comparable to competitors in the area for this type of work, you're off to a good start.

Many companies have a formal new-employee orientation program, and perhaps it's time to rethink yours—that is, if it is done by seating the new worker alone in a room to watch a video or using an interactive computer program that contains mostly boring details like how vacation time is accrued and where the first-aid kits are located in each department. It's not that this information is unimportant, but employee loyalty and commitment can be shown from the first day on the job, simply by assigning a friendly coworker to shepherd the process—answer questions, show the new person around, have lunch with him or her, and so on. Even the employee handbook should be written and presented in

## TRAINING THE NEW EMPLOYEE . . .
## TO FEEL VALUABLE

The way people process information dictates how they learn. If you deliver information to your staff in a variety of ways—written and spoken, logical and creative—you will enable each individual to absorb knowledge and master skills in the most productive way.

- Involve all associates in training activities and discussions. Conduct exercises to develop skills in such areas as displaying merchandise, writing sales slips, entering point-of-sale data, and stating sales goals. Invite participation in weekly store meetings and impromptu sales floor discussions.

- Team up new associates with more experienced members of your staff for the first few weeks. They'll appreciate the opportunity to observe each other.

- Ask new staffers to report their observations and submit suggestions as they learn about different areas in the store. This will help them be creative and feel involved. Then let them try some of their ideas.

- Ask new associates to review records or reports, or to research topics important to your business. For example, ask them to compare competitors' repair prices, or have them inventory your supplies and prepare an order for the upcoming month based on past sales history. Their analysis not only may facilitate their learning but may also lead to some logical changes for your store.

- Observe new associates with customers and provide them with feedback immediately. Reinforce skills and provide information that is lacking. Review store procedures.

- Monitor your new associates' progress with a checklist and planned meetings. An organized checklist that clearly states what you expect employees to master ensures that you do not overlook important considerations, and enables you to review progress according to a training plan. Your checklist should include selling skills and operational areas like security, service, and display in addition to product knowledge.

*Source:* Janice Mack Talcott and Kate B. Peterson, Performance Concepts, Olympia, Washington, in *JCK* (Jewelers Circular Keystone), July 1998 issue. *JCK* is a publication of Cahners Business Information. ©Cahners.

an easy-to-read and easy-to-handle format, rather than a giant notebook full of intimidating legal terminology or poorly photocopied forms.

Increasingly, companies are also deciding that orientation is not a onetime or first-day event, but can be accomplished over a longer time period—say, the first week or first month—broken into more manageable topics, with occasional refresher courses on subjects like benefits, workplace safety, and so on. Schedule regular check-ins with workers one, two, three, and four months after their hire dates, to ask how things are going. Their feedback may prompt improvements or additions to the orientation system.

## STRUCTURE DRIVES BEHAVIOR

This should be no surprise to anyone who's ever been employed: Our work environment has a significant influence on the way we act. With this in mind, what do new employees see as they view their new surroundings, and what conclusions might they draw from these observations? Managers would do well to look at their stores through these "new" eyes.

If the system rewards competitiveness among coworkers, we'll be competitive, even if the internal memos are all touting harmony and teamwork. If the system punishes us when we don't "do it right the first time," we'll do everything in our power not to mess up—even if we have to leave good ideas and great experiments by the wayside. If the system and its associated structures—things like performance appraisal, promotion practices, and bonus programs—discourage attacks on the status quo, we'll learn rather quickly to keep our mouths shut.

The system and the structures it creates drive behavior, often to the point where very different people in an organization end up acting alike over time. Not only do they behave in similar ways, they frequently share the same frustrations. How many times have you heard statements like these from coworkers?

- "Sure, I'd like to try a new way, but if it doesn't work out, my career will be down the tubes."
- "I wouldn't normally handle it this way—but in this company, it's either their way or the highway."
- "Those are great ideas, but I'm not the one to talk to about them. You'd better check with my boss; she's the only one authorized to make any changes."

Even more insidious than dictating what we can't or don't do, the system—as revealed by the behaviors it rewards and the actions it supports—instructs us what to do. For example, despite any number of customer service initiatives, call center employees may still be rushing through customer calls because they are being rewarded based on the number of calls they handle in a given time period. Because awards or bonuses are still awarded on an individual basis, each salesperson may continue to operate like the Lone Ranger, though the salesperson is fully aware that the company would derive greater benefit if he or she cooperated with other members of the team. Despite a card in his wallet that lists "Respect for all employees" as a company value, a manager still chews someone out in front of his coworkers, and gets away with it.

Managers who want to shape a more intrinsically supportive environment must analyze which of the structures in the system may actually demotivate the workers. In any organization, the devil is rarely in the details. It is in the structures that underlie them.

## Getting Back to Basics

One of the most frustrating aspects for managers in retail and service industries is that creating a "supportive environment" necessitates starting at the very beginning in terms of skill building for workers with little or no employment experience. The part-time quick-service restaurant worker, for instance, may have to be taught basic etiquette and customer service skills. This is why so many food service businesses use "canned" phrases ("Welcome to Burger King . . .") that can be memorized and parroted to every customer. The theory is that "canned" courtesy is better than no courtesy at all! Or at least, it's a start.

It is important to realize that first steps are just that—first steps on the path to motivating novice workers. When they know what to do, how to do it, and why they are doing it, they gain confidence along with their skills. These are not the kinds of jobs for which managers can dangle advancement opportunities, bigger commissions, and corner offices as perks for outstanding performance. Instead, a good manager serves more of a mentoring role in these situations, teaching the cornerstones—mutual respect, responsibility, trust, and honesty—as well as customer service skills. Every employee appreciates (and expects) the opportunity to learn and grow, even more so in entry-level positions. A manager's job is to find and present those opportunities and keep 'em coming. Along the way, instill pride in their successes. You may be grooming the next store manager, district manager, or owner of the chain! It's a matter of time and patience . . . and everybody starts somewhere.

## WHY WORKERS LEAVE

Workplace relationships are based on the individual and collective behavior of the people who make up that workplace. If the structures largely dictate behavior within the system, it is our humanness that dictates the nature and power of these relationships. Individual workers' personalities and intellects come into play in most jobs, and so do their emotions. In fact, emotions are at the heart of many resignations and/or new job searches.

However, before we delve into the reasons that people leave, let's talk about the reasons they choose to stay at a particular company:

- They feel their work is meaningful. They are challenged by it and interested in it. They understand where their job "fits" in terms of the company hierarchy, and they feel their role is important to the company's success as well as their own career success.
- They feel that they are trusted. They are given the responsibility and autonomy necessary to meet deadlines and make decisions—decisions that are not constantly second-guessed. If they want to know something, they don't feel intimidated asking about it. The company is good about sharing information—good and bad news alike—and makes communication a priority.
- They have a comfort level with coworkers they like and trust. Their store or department just "clicks," because the people get along and work well together.
- They know they are compensated fairly for what they do. This encompasses more than wages; it also includes benefits, acknowledgment of work/life issues, and opportunities to learn new skills.
- Depending on the particular job and individual, they see this position as part of a bigger picture, a necessary step on the career path for themselves and a place to learn skills that will allow them to move forward—either in this organization or the next.
- Conversely, since more than half of retail industry workers are part-timers, they appreciate the company's ability to offer them flexible work hours, seasonal schedules, employee discounts, and other benefits unique to the retail trade. Some simply love the business, or the merchandise, look, and feel of the store in which they work. They are service-oriented and enjoy the personal contact with customers and coworkers.
- They work for a company that they are proud of and/or a manager they respect and admire. If they are on a career development path, this company looks good on their résumé because of its training and advancement opportunities and overall reputation for excellence.

Of course, not all of these reasons apply to every employee. Their motivations are different depending on their circumstances. As retail training specialists Kate B. Peterson and Janice Mack Talcott of Performance Concepts put it, managers should "start by recognizing that you cannot motivate anyone to do anything! Everyone is motivated, but people do things for their own reasons, not yours."[3]

It is often said that employees don't leave jobs or companies—they leave their managers. It is perhaps ironic that a magazine based in India quotes a survey of 1,400 retail executives and managers in the United States, with these eye-opening results:

- 42 percent of those surveyed would leave their present jobs to follow a "good boss" rather than build a new relationship with his or her successor.
- 84 percent like what they do for a living—but not where they do it.
- 81 percent feel that "the way to the top" is political in their companies.
- 76 percent said they'd leave their present job for less money, to work for a company that offers greater personal development and flexibility.[4]

Add those results to another, even more recent survey. From the report "Retail Workers 2005" by CareerBuilder.com:

- 48 percent of retail workers said they don't look forward to going to work each day, and they feel "excessive stress" on the job.
- 35 percent say they struggle to maintain a healthy work/life balance.
- 67 percent say their workloads increased "significantly" in the previous six months.[5]

What stands out in each of the survey responses is that, while some are fact-based and could be specifically proven (increased workloads, for instance)—all of them focus on what people are *feeling*, which is just as valid but harder to define.

Although most managers would agree that the people who work for them have strong emotions, many leaders certainly never hear the kinds of complaints offered in those surveys, and honestly don't realize that such a high percentage of their workforce is miserable. More often, companies operate as if their employees can choose to leave their feelings at home when they come to work. For instance, do you believe that people can (and should) separate feelings from analytical abilities and strive to make purely objective judgments? Do you believe that expressions of emotion in the workplace are inappropriate? Would you depend on people to be logical in their business dealings?

At work, we're told to "stick to the facts" and "leave our emotions out of the discussion." The assumption seems to be that to be productive, intelligent people should learn to limit expression of their fears, hopes, anxieties, and excitement. The problem with this way of thinking is that it is unrealistic. Humans are always affected by our emotions, whether we choose to be or not. Even when we suppress them success-fully, other emotions surface—resentment, anger, and so on. And even when we are shown hard data to prove that what we're complaining about isn't as widespread or problematic as we believe, it does not en-tirely erase our own negative feelings. More likely, it creates more emo-tions, including mistrust, cynicism, and embarrassment about stating a complaint, only to be shown that it's "not really valid."

While the humanness of the system adds complexity, with this com-plexity comes the opportunity for sharp managers to design systems that deepen commitment and improve morale. The best managers don't just "manage" their people—they understand what drives their people and *develop* them based on their own skills, desires, and career goals. All of this involves attention to the whole person, not just the warm body who happens to be filling the position. It is a longer and more involved pro-cess than can be described in this book.

There's not much enthusiasm for employee development in retail, other than perhaps with a few sales "stars." Most managers would tell you they have their hands full. It's all they can do to schedule workers, order supplies, and juggle meetings and the employees' various "per-sonal crises." Little wonder that the four most common complaints peo-ple have about their workplace (from human resource consultant and author Scott Hunter) indicate a lack of management development skills:

1. "My boss doesn't recognize, respect, or reward my efforts."
2. "Why do people spend so much time gossiping and talking behind each others' backs?"
3. "All the company cares about is money."
4. "I hate it when the higher-ups make major policy changes, never con-sidering how they will impact the people who get the work done."[6]

Again, please note that each statement is more a matter of personal feeling and perception, and not necessarily fact. As a manager, how would you go about combating each of these gripes—in a way that prompts a *positive feeling* from the complainer, not just a quick resolu-tion for the department or company? Here are some thoughts to prompt the discussion:

- In a larger retail organization, senior management may be dropping the ball in communicating strategies, plans, and expectations to mid-dle or department managers—the ones who are expected to explain the "big picture" (why it got that way, and how it works) to front-line employees, and who are also more likely to encounter the fallout when things don't go well.

- If you ask for feedback and receive it, you must be prepared to act on it. Among the most frustrating things to workers is the manager who appears to care, by asking questions and claiming he or she is going to "get to the bottom of it," whatever "it" is. The employees are concise and candid in their responses—but time passes and nothing changes. If there is a valid reason you are unable to address a specific issue, share this information with the employees. Otherwise, there is no reason to solicit feedback or suggestions and then ignore them. Doing so can make you look even worse in the eyes of already disgruntled workers.[7]

## THE ROLE OF CHANGE

Many employee departures are some type of reaction to change. Think about it: A new manager is hired, with a whole new style to adapt to, and some subordinates would rather leave than try. The store is sold to new owners. Several coworkers leave, and their close friends who remain say things "just aren't the same" without them. A person accepts a transfer rather than being laid off, only to find that the new job isn't as interesting or meaningful to them. An elderly parent suddenly requires full-time care, and somebody's got to tend to it, job or no job. Change is everywhere, but that doesn't make it any easier to deal with.

Even the workplace system itself has a tendency toward self-protection in the face of change. In reshaping it to encourage everyone's best efforts, try to change the way the system performs—push at it or pull at it in any direction—and it resists. As managers learn the hard way, resistance to change is often directed personally at the individual(s) thought to be the source of the change, and the grumblings and rumors begin to fly. It's almost like the system is producing the equivalent of white blood cells to fight off infection. Across departments, people—consciously and unconsciously, directly and subtly—protect the sense of order and predictability in the organization as they know it. This is especially true among those who have succeeded under the old structure—the top sales associate, for example, who resists any changes to the compensation plan or commission structure. Surprisingly, those who have not been as successful in the old structure—including some who openly claim to detest it—are also frequently among the most vociferous in resisting change. They'd simply rather fight than switch.

## Systems Thinking

Most of us still tend to underestimate the creativity and commitment of our coworkers and therefore fail to capture the full potential of the workforce in renewal and reinvention efforts. And yet, only with allied coworkers who understand the system does a company have a true opportunity to improve it.

Over the past half century, there has been a growing tendency to describe organizations and tasks as systems, much as we did in the first part of this chapter in the discussion of retention as a process. Yet there is still considerable resistance to this type of thinking in American corporations. It's not really a criticism; managers and employees are simply more comfortable with the traditional view of the organization, where the focus is on certainty and predictability and on managing individual elements. It is difficult to understand and deal with the complex interrelationships that define an open, organic, constantly adapting system.

What today's managers risk is oversimplifying a system that is, in fact, a variety of highly interactive parts and pieces, in which decisions made in one store or department in a chain may have unintended effects on others.

It isn't always possible to focus on the entire system when trying to improve morale, solve problems, and retain the good employee who is sitting right in front of us! Nor should we always try. Just as scientists sometimes focus on atoms, molecules, or compounds, depending on what they are investigating, retail managers can focus on individuals, work groups, teams, departments, functional areas, sales channels, and so on, at different times. If we can develop better methods for understanding these groups as well as the relationships among them, we may be better able to understand why the behavior in an organization is frequently different from what we think it ought to be.

Understanding only the "parts and pieces" is simply too limiting.

The next step is managing the systems to meet employees' needs, creating the kind of workplace that excites and challenges them, welcoming ideas and treating people fairly. Realistically, what is the alternative in an industry already fraught with turnover problems?

Attorneys Teresa Demchak and Barry Goldstein of the California law firm Goldstein, Demchak, Baller, Borgen & Dardarian specialize in workplace litigation, from civil rights violations to employment discrimination and wage and hour lawsuits. In a 2004 research paper, they outlined some of the most common (and costliest) mistakes employers make. A few involve retention and motivation issues, because they deal with employment and advancement policies—but notice that in all cases, effective *systems* could have solved these problems:

- The employer does not effectively deal with historical practices or stereotypes that may limit the employment opportunities for minorities or women.
- The employer does not ensure that its selection practices are actually related to hiring, promoting, or training persons who are likely to be better performers on the job.
- The employer does not establish systems for determining and taking advantage of the actual job interests and ambitions of its employees.
- The employer does not adequately manage the employment consequences of a rapidly changing workforce caused by acquisition, expansion, or downsizing.[8]

Ultimately, these are morale issues long before they become legal issues. This highly respected law firm suggests extensive planning—and reminds executives that even the best plans on paper mean little in court if they were not implemented, or were implemented only partially or inadequately.

## LEARNING FROM GOODBYES

Even under the best circumstances, people leave their jobs for a variety of reasons. Before they get out the door, you have one final opportunity to learn from their experience. This is why having an exit interview process is so important. It is too late to ask the employee to stay, or to "make right" whatever they felt was wrong (if that's why they say they're leaving). But it is never too late to get honest feedback that may pinpoint problems with your existing systems or policies.

Some managers are concerned about exit interviews. They can be uncomfortable, and soon-to-be former employees may not be "really honest" about their gripes (especially personality conflicts) if they expect a reference from the manager in the future. But Nobscot Corporation, a company that specializes in exit interview software for managers, says most departing employees appreciate the chance to let management know where problems exist. They still have emotional ties to the company, and if handled correctly, an exit interview gives them a chance to make a final contribution. It can be handled by e-mail, if necessary, or a third party (other than the person's former supervisor) can do the interview.

An objective interviewer is important, because he or she is not just listening to one employee's complaints but looking for patterns, themes, and trends. Over time, the information should be tracked and used to develop recommendations for improvements.

The Society for Human Resource Management (SHRM) says 9 out of 10 companies now conduct some form of exit interview. If you're the one who must conduct them—or if someone else conducts them and you're not allowed to be there—the tips in the box, "How to Conduct In-person Exit Interviews," should give you some ideas about what goes on in a productive exit interview.

The final point, number 6, is a good ending spot for this chapter because it also refers to the single most critical thing managers must do

## HOW TO CONDUCT IN-PERSON EXIT INTERVIEWS

1. Have exit interviews done by a third party (HR or other) and not with the supervisor in attendance. The goal is to get honest communication. The pluses and the minuses. With the supervisor in attendance, chances are slim that the exiting employee will speak up on any important issues.

2. Conduct exit interviews for areas/departments where you "smell" trouble. If there happens to be a lot of turnover in one area, that's a red-flag to start exit-interviewing all departing employees from that area. (You may want to even interview non-departing employees as well.)

3. Have questions preplanned. You should have a standard list of questions that you ask on each exit interview. Find out what they liked best and least, how they would rate their supervisor, the compensation, benefits, etc. Give them the opportunity to offer suggestions for improvement.

4. Take information received seriously, but with a grain of salt. Don't allow one negative employee to disrupt your whole organization. Look for patterns in exit interview responses. Share the information tactfully with supervisors. Make action plans to verify serious issues. Work on improving the negatives.

5. Don't let the ex-employee go on and on and on. The exit interview should take 15–20 minutes. You don't get any more info by hearing the employee whine about every last detail. Just like an employment interview, learn how to get the information you need, and send them on their way.

6. Thank them for their service. One small step that you can make on behalf of your company is to thank them for what they have done during their employment. Many employees are never thanked. It means a lot.

each and every day for people under their supervision: remember to say "thanks." Nothing goes quite so far in motivating or retaining employees as simply letting them know that their work is appreciated.

## CHAPTER SUMMARY

The extremely high turnover in the retail industry makes employee retention efforts all the more critical. Turnover has an impact on morale (and the workload) of the people who remain, as well as creating additional costs for finding and training replacements.

It may not be a manager's job to keep employees "happy," but it is in both the manager's and the company's best interest to have employees who are interested in and challenged by their jobs. This chapter covered the subject of how to retain good employees by meeting their needs and developing their skills—a real challenge when every person comes to work with different needs and skills, along with his or her own motivations and reasons for working at the company.

This chapter urged management to view retention as a process that begins with hiring the "right" person for a job, and continues by setting the stage for a good first impression with a friendly orientation to the company. The chapter described how workers learn how they're "supposed to act" from the workplace environment, and that too few workplaces are energizing and motivating.

Reasons for staying at a company—and for choosing to leave—were examined, using recent retail-industry surveys to point out pervasive problems. The key role that people's emotions play in their jobs is clearly shown, with advice for managers about how to take the "whole person" into account. The challenge of creating a positive management style for entry-level workers, and the natural resistance to change, were also discussed. The chapter ended with a look at the importance of exit interviews as a tool to improve the system for employees who remain.

## DISCUSSION QUESTIONS

**1.** Why do you think turnover is so high in the retail industry, and what would you do about it as a store owner? As a store manager whose owner is notoriously "cheap"?

2. Do you think it is employees' natural tendency when they get together (or work closely on a regular basis) to complain about their
working conditions? Is that fair to their employer? What can companies do about on-the-job cynics and "complainers"?

3. How is motivating an entry-level worker different from motivating
an experienced one?

4. Why is it necessary to think of workplace retention issues in terms
of "systems"?

5. Describe how and why you left your last job, and how your departure was handled by your employer. Knowing what you now know,
how could the process have been improved? (Alternately, interview
another person about his or her last "job departure" and answer the
same questions about it based on his or her impressions.)

## ENDNOTES

1. Tabulation and analysis of U.S. Bureau of Labor Statistics data, Employment
Policy Foundation, Washington, D.C., October 22, 2004.

2. See endnote 1.

3. Janice Mack Talcott and Kate B. Peterson, "Finding the Staffer with the Right
Stuff," *JCK* (Jewelers' Circular Keystone) magazine, ©Cahners Business Information, Cambridge, Massachusetts, July 1998.

4. Rajesh Kaushik and Anurag Chandra, "Scoring High," *The Times of India*, June
2004.

5. "Retail Workers 2005" survey results from CareerBuilder.com, quoted in *Entrepreneurial Connection*, the online newsletter of the National Association for the
Self-Employed, North Richland Hills, Texas, February 2005.

6. Scott Hunter, *Making Work Work*, (Irvine, CA: Hunter Alliance Press, 2003),
quoted in *Entrepreneurial Connection*, the online newsletter of the National Association for the Self-Employed, North Richland Hills, Texas, February 2005.

7. B. Carvin, "Be Prepared to Act Once You Ask," Nobscot Corporation, Honolulu,
Hawaii, ©B. Carvin, 2000.

8. Barry Goldstein and Teresa Demchak, "The Most Significant Mistakes Made by
Employers from a Plaintiff's Attorney's Perspective," ©Goldstein, Demchak,
Baller, Borgen & Dardarian, April 2004.

# BUILDING CORE
# VALUES

Over the past few decades, there has been a gradual undermining of many organizations and institutions that people have traditionally turned to for a sense of belonging. There's been a notable deemphasis on the extended family, and even the nuclear family has been diminished by separation and divorce. Many have fallen away from religion when they saw its leaders not practicing what they preached. Many more have become cynical about government when the self-serving actions of elected officials were revealed, or when the programs they counted on were dropped, underfunded, or no longer appeared to work. Longtime political affiliations have also been weakened as the major parties have adopted platforms that seem more like a response to trends than a reflection of their members' strongly held beliefs.

More and more of our traditional institutions have become harder to believe in. What does this mean for our corporate institutions—and the people who work for them?

In this chapter, we examine what retailers can do to build and keep reputations for being both ethical and community-minded. Included are the following topics:

- Core values and why they are important
- How values apply to retailing
- Values to expect from employees
- Components of corporate citizenship

Disappointment in our traditional institutions notwithstanding, people all over America are looking for something worthwhile to do with their lives and skills. If this weren't the case, why do one-third of us find the time to volunteer more than three hours a week to charitable causes outside the workplace? Why do many of us work harder for that volunteer organization than we do for the one that pays us?

These questions go to the very heart of the issues involved in remaking the workplace into one that is intrinsically uplifting and motivating. Collectively, we are a people seeking something powerful and meaningful to touch our hearts and minds. We do not respond for long to small-minded people with self-centered purposes. Most of us are at our best when we are swept up by commitment and working in the service of a larger goal. We're looking for a cause that fires our imagination and excites our spirit. For the organization that can satisfy these needs—particularly when there is a dearth of organizations that can—an enormous opportunity exists to create loyal, satisfied employees. But how does today's retailer tap into this type of enthusiasm?

## REGAINING TRUST

Many people view corporations with cynicism and mistrust, no matter what the industry. One major study of business ethics was released in 1999, when the nonprofit public policy research group the Hudson Institute teamed up with Walker Information, a corporate research firm, to survey more than 3,000 U.S. workers in 48 states. All were at least 18 years old, some part-timers and some full-timers, in workplaces with at least 50 employees. They represented a cross section of industries, government, and nonprofit organizations, and their answers were weighted based on current U.S. labor statistics.

What did these employees say when asked about the ethical conduct of their employers?

- 60 percent of employees said their organization is "highly ethical," but only 47 percent described their leadership that way.
- 25 percent were neutral on the subject, and 16 percent did not believe their workplace is highly ethical.
- 30 percent said they either knew of or suspected unethical behavior in their workplaces over the past two years, but 60 percent who knew about or witnessed an ethical violation did not report it.[1]

The retail industry scored in the middle of the survey on most topics but stood out for its high numbers of ethical violations, about half of which were related to employee theft. This was a higher incidence than any other industry, but retail employees were also more comfortable reporting violations, and the majority believes that management handles these allegations well.[2]

The survey results underscore the need for core values that a company shows to the world and to its employees. But exactly what are "core values"?

## Getting to the Core

A company's values are its code of ethics, its behavioral framework. Taken together, they form a statement of what the organization collectively deems important or valuable—what it stands for. When understood and adopted by employees, values provide a context for action. Values can provide a sense of order without rules, reduce ambiguity without a detailed plan, and bring focus and coherence while allowing individual expression and self-determination. Values must be every organization's North Star—an ever-visible guide that employees can look to, in order to tell whether they are acting in ways that promote the organizational good.

To be effective, values must be

- Profound enough to touch the hearts and minds of all employees, yet simple enough to be readily understood
- Concrete enough to provide a useful framework for decision making

- Pragmatic enough and sufficiently consistent with organizational structures to be reinforced in normal day-to-day activities
- Communicated over time, in every aspect of the business
- Reinforced through accountability

Most organizations do have a published set of values, or code of conduct. They are usually well written and widely communicated . . . and are a significant source of frustration. Why? Because it is a rare company today in which people practice the values their organization preaches. Just listen to the grumbling at coffee breaks, read between the lines at the next employee meeting, or read the comments on the employee surveys—the gap between our professed values and our values in practice is significant. A few examples:

- If respecting the individual is a core value, why do we promote so many people who are technical experts but have lousy people skills? And why do we tolerate managers who get results but are frequently disrespectful to people in their work groups?
- If we value cooperation and teamwork, why have we designed so many structures that reward people for competing more than cooperating?
- If every employee is encouraged to seek excellence, then why do we still have so many uninteresting, narrowly defined jobs?
- Why is training the first thing to be cut when money is tight?
- If providing the best possible service to customers is a core value, then why do we make so many rules that make it hard for employees to meet customers' needs?
- If we have adopted a Total Quality approach, why are so few senior managers actively involved in the effort?

. . . and the list goes on. A company's failure to measure the extent to which its employees (especially its managers) live the espoused values has made it easy for many to overlook how often they do not "walk the talk." The result has been lower levels of trust, greater confusion and frustration, and less sense of community among employees in many organizations. People genuinely want their company to stand for something.

The first step in closing the gap as it relates to values is to choose to get serious about doing so. Look at the values that are already on paper. Were they written decades ago? Just how committed is the company to acting within this framework? If a person purposely acts in a manner inconsistent with these values, what is the likely consequence? Dismissal? Coach and counsel? For most, it's an easy decision when an employee

## ONE COMPANY'S CORE VALUES

*BD (Becton, Dickinson and Company)*

BD of Franklin Lakes, New Jersey, is a medical technology company, but its core values could easily be adapted for retailers—or any other type of organization:

*We treat each other with respect.*

BD associates act with respect toward each other and toward those with whom we interact. We disagree openly and honestly, and we deal with our differences professionally. Once we have made a decision, we act together in harmony.

*We do what is right.*

We are committed to the highest standards of excellence in everything that we do: on behalf of our customers, our shareholders, our communities, and ourselves. We are proud to work for a health care company whose products and services make a difference in people's lives. We derive our greatest sense of accomplishment from doing what is right—not what is expedient. We are reliable, honest, and trust-worthy in all our dealings. We keep our promises and if we make a mistake, we put it right.

*We always seek to improve.*

Superior quality is the "ground floor" of our organization. Upon it we continually strive to improve by developing, manufacturing and supplying products and services superior to our competitors' and better than the previous one. We study our progress and learn from ourselves and others how to do things more effectively and efficiently. Our commitment to quality goes beyond how well we serve our customers to include the way we deal with all people. How we do things is as important as what we do.

*We accept personal responsibility.*

We consider individual involvement and accountability to be both a right and a privilege and accept personal responsibility for everything we do. We treat the company's reputation as our own and try to make wise use of our time and the company's resources. We expect access to the tools and information necessary to participate in any decisions that will reflect on our collective or individual reputations.

*Source:* Becton, Dickinson and Company, Franklin Lakes, New Jersey, 2005. ©BD; used with the company's permission.

steals from the company. But what if one of the core values is "respect"— and a longtime supervisor is clearly and consistently disrespectful of employees in situations clearly witnessed by coworkers?

In cases of infractions, how many "second chances" does a person get? If there isn't significant accountability for the clear and deliberate abuse of values, then there are no values. On the other hand, when action is taken—when people who don't live the values are asked to leave—there is usually little, if any, follow-up to reinforce the message and consequences. Instead . . . there is silence.

The only thing worse than not having a set of guidelines to provide order to behavior within a system is to have a visible set of values that are situationally enforced or largely ignored.

## Telling the (Partial) Truth

One of the reasons it is difficult to pinpoint values-related problems—for instance, to get people to report ethics infractions—is that the organizational deck is stacked, so to speak, against managers. When we are liked, people often color the information they give us because they don't want to disappoint us and/or they don't want to complain. If they fear our reaction (either because of our past actions or our position), very little information about the less-than-positive aspects of the current situation is volunteered. Most of us have felt the pressure not to be "too negative," or to balance positive information with any "bad news." The expression "*YOU* tell the boss" didn't evolve because people were reluctant to be rewarded, but because they didn't want to experience the boss's wrath!

And it's not just a matter of how to tell the boss. People have a general bias toward seeing things as they wish things were, not as they actually are. The choice to avoid the truth is not always a conscious one and is often quite subtle. So bad news doesn't travel "up" quickly in most organizations—although it should. By sugarcoating and selectively modifying reality, we falsely diminish people's understanding of "the gap" and therefore rob the organization of the sense of urgency and creative tension that will be required to focus and sustain improvement efforts, let alone report problems.

The National Business Ethics Study cited at the beginning of this chapter noted three primary reasons people did not report misconduct by fellow workers, even when they had personally witnessed it:

- They didn't feel the organization would respond.
- There was a perceived lack of anonymous and confidential means of reporting.
- They feared retaliation from management.[3]

Developing a shared sense of reality must be a strategic issue. It is exceedingly difficult to change reality if people don't see it, or if there is no agreement on what "real" is. We must recognize the effect the business structure has on our willingness and ability to see reality, and we must search out and eliminate those practices that make it safer or more rewarding to do anything but "tell it like it is."

## RETAIL-SPECIFIC VALUES

Core values guide more than employee behavior. They also guide customers' impressions of the business. Of course, a retailer cannot count on every customer to have looked on its Web site at the "Core Values" page; nor can employees stand at the doors and pass out copies to incoming shoppers. So how does the message come through?

Core values in the retail industry involve the way people deal with customers as well as coworkers. These are topics like convenience and customer service, as well as types of products that are chosen for sale, how they are merchandised, and how they are priced. Each of these has a component that can reflect the message: "We care about what our customers want. That's why we do it this way."

"Values create value," says Dr. Leonard L. Berry, Distinguished Professor of Marketing and founder of the Center for Retailing Studies at Texas A&M University. Berry explains the retail connection this way:

> People like to associate with others who share their values, including companies. By touching customers' hearts through their excellence, authenticity, uniqueness, spirit, generosity, and caring, retailers can penetrate customer skepticism and guardedness. They can establish feelings of closeness, trust, and even affection. Retailers whose core values reflect customers' personal ideals and principles of living are most likely to create compelling value for customers. Customers respond to companies that care about them as human beings.[4]

Living these values in the retail environment is possible only with well-trained and well-informed employees. Uninformed, partially committed employees cannot be expected to deliver on deadline, meet sales quotas, and ensure customer loyalty. On the other hand, if our organizations provide employees with interesting work, sufficient training, and the opportunity to reach their potential, the chances are excellent that they will make the commitment.

The fact is that most retail jobs have not been designed to produce value for the customer while also providing opportunities for the personal or professional development of the employee. In a large percentage of cases, just the opposite is true. We've designed jobs in ways that make sense from an efficiency standpoint—to sell the most merchandise profitably and clear out the rest—but they do little to feed people's needs to learn, grow, and be challenged. In the short run (quarterly sales figures), the current system may even seem effective. However, as an organization increasingly calls on its people to look sharp, make suggestions, and outsmart the competition, the price being paid for doing things "the way they've always been done" is already too steep.

The question is this: Is it possible to create an interesting, challenging job for every employee? Can a company really organize so that every worker has a chance to grow and prosper? And, more to the point, is it even possible to accomplish this without turning the store hierarchy completely on end?

Certainly, not all jobs are equally interesting or appealing. This is particularly true in inherently unchallenging, highly repetitive, low-paying, little-experience-required jobs, of which there are probably millions in the retail trade. However, even in most of these jobs, interest and commitment are possible for many employees if, in addition to performing the tasks, they are charged with management of the process.

What would this entail? Here are eight responsibilities to consider that will build the foundation for process improvement efforts:

1. **Gather customer information.** In the normal course of business, employees should regularly ask customers what they like or don't like about the company's products and services, and what they'd like to see done differently. This information can be promptly analyzed and communicated throughout the organization.

2. **Help design the service delivery process.** In retail, this involves multiple facets of the business, from display to POS systems and policies, to how to handle special orders, returns, irate customers, and the like—which means the employee must understand the *entire* delivery process, not just the job that he or she performs. Everyone must accept the implications of their work and have the ability to influence the way that work is accomplished.

3. **Customize the process when necessary.** Why is it that some employees don't act in the customer's best interest when common sense often dictates a different, obvious course of action? Often, it's because many employees today still aren't trusted to make even the simplest deviations in the process and must get supervisory approval to do so. For an organization to be considered truly responsive, this must change.

4. **Measure the quality of their own performance.** The primary benefit to be gained here is that the direct, unfiltered feedback employees

receive enhances their learning. Whether employees are or aren't allowed to measure their own performance is often an issue of trust. Many managers believe that employees are unable to, and haven't been trained to, measure their performance effectively—and surely they wouldn't voluntarily identify their own weaknesses, would they? Wouldn't they be honest in their self-appraisal if fear were eliminated from the process?

5. **Identify disgruntled customers.** Often, the customers we lose are the ones who are marginally dissatisfied but are not particularly vocal about it. Most customers don't complain; they just move on. Customer-contact employees can often head off such losses if they are given the responsibility to seek out those quiet, unhappy customers, and the authority to do something to alleviate the causes of dissatisfaction quickly.

6. **Find the root cause of service problems.** In most service companies, management controls the process, and only a few people analyze information and figure out how to solve problems. Many retailers still claim that they can't "afford" to give employees time to meet for an hour at the end of every week to discuss what they learned that week and to set priorities for improvements in the coming week. But if it improves sales and morale and empowers the employees, why not make the time?

7. **Improve the process.** Innovation and continuous improvement of processes have not traditionally been responsibilities of most employees. There is a significant difference between performing a task and playing a part in managing a process. The former can get repetitive quickly; the latter is continually engaging.

8. **Have the power to routinely eliminate non-value-adding tasks.** In most organizations, almost everyone has some unproductive activities on their to-do lists. Typically, only managers can choose to eliminate these tasks. Why? If we respect people's minds, why don't we trust them to get rid of activities that waste their time—or at least build a process that enables them to point out wasteful activities without fear of retaliation?

## Personal Values

We've talked a lot about what companies can do for their workers to make them feel valued and challenged. But shouldn't the workers themselves have some duty to uphold the company's core values, as well as their own? Their personal attitudes and motivations will make all the difference in a retail environment. Again, Dr. Leonard Berry of Texas A&M University puts it succinctly:

> Inspiring retail employees is critical because they are in some ways "volunteer workers." Employees choose whether or not to give more effort than the amount required to earn a commission or bonus or to avoid a penalty; they choose whether or not to volunteer extra effort. Volunteerism is an important idea in retailing because every retailer creates value for customers through the human performances we call service. Customers notice a "can-do" service attitude when they experience it—and also a "can't do" attitude.[5]

To use Dr. Berry's analogy, how does one find "good volunteers?" Internationally known author, speaker, and professional coach—literally, he *is* a former coach, of the Cal State Fullerton football team—Bob Davies cites three principles he believes workers must live by for their company to be, in Davies's words, "living in integrity." With his kind permission, we share them here, along with Davies's abbreviated comments about each:

1. **I do what I say I will do.** I can't tell you how many times I have heard an individual say that they were committed to reach some goal and then not take the intended actions. They all had viable reasons, stories, priorities, unscheduled interruptions, and excuses. They all also didn't do what they said they would do! If an individual had set a smaller, more realistic goal, then they would still maintain hope, and the chance to be successful and honor Principle #1. I'm not against setting stretch goals. I simply request that you also determine a bottom line that you *give your word* you will achieve, no matter what. Try it!

2. **I can't do it by myself. I am far better off as part of a team than I can ever be alone.** Elite performers will never argue with this. They know that they must surround themselves with others. By doing so, they create the atmosphere where learning, discovery, clarity, and accountability can occur.

3. **I am the source of all that I experience.** The opposite of accountability is blaming. This principle is a source of strength for people. It doesn't allow them to become victims; it embraces the concept that human beings are very powerful at creating results in their own lives. These may be dysfunctional results, however! Someone who has financial difficulties, for example, has exactly what they should have, given their current financial point of view. If they want to have different results, it is not what is going on around them—the environment, the marketplace, etc. The answer lies in their own dysfunctional point

of view. If they want to change the results they are experiencing, they must first change their point of view.[6]

Davies goes on to advise how to change that point of view, information you can receive from his books or on his Web site (www.bobdavies .com)

## The Customers Care, Too

At the risk of exaggerating to make the point, would you want to be in a personal or even a business relationship with a manager who berates the people who work with him? Probably not. Most of us have winced when we've seen a tyrannical boss in action, spreading fear and loathing throughout the organization. The abusive boss is a staple of comic strips, cartoons, and sitcoms—but in real life, the situation may be sad, uncomfortable, embarrassing, infuriating; it is certainly not funny.

So if and when customers hear stories about how your company is difficult to work for and how tough your employees have it—or heaven help you, if they witness someone's tirade on the sales floor—they might just decide to find some other store to visit in the future. Call it optimistic thinking, but most people believe that the company that treats its own people well will do the same for its customers.

Along those same lines, the way a company treats its employees will filter down to the way those employees treat customers. As you've probably seen time and again in families, in classrooms, or on the job, people in a given social setting will model the values and behaviors they see.

What are they seeing in your store?

## CORPORATE CITIZENSHIP

Information cuts both ways. At the same time retailers are doing market research to learn about their customers, the customers are learning more about the companies with which they do business. Retailers aren't just in the advertisements every day. When they lay off employees, when they're involved in a lawsuit, when profits are up or down—all of these routinely make news. So do interesting or unique new products, the company's support of charities and event sponsorships, and its enlightened policies about protecting natural resources, to name a few.

Today's customers are more inclined than ever before to make purchasing decisions based on whether they believe a particular company is socially responsible or not. In the 2004 Cone Corporation Citizenship Study of 1,033 consumers nationwide:

- 90 percent said they would consider no longer purchasing goods or services from a company that had "a negative citizenship track record"
- 92 percent said companies should be "more socially responsible" in light of scandals at Enron and other corporations
- 77 percent said, "companies have a responsibility to help support causes," through charitable donations and other efforts
- 43 percent said they had purchased a product in the past year after hearing about the company's commitment to a social cause[7]

None of this should surprise companies interested in building customer relationships. As half of that relationship, the customer wants to feel good about who you are and the way you do business. Depending on their own values, this may mean they expect any or all of the following priorities—and remember, as a retailer, these also apply to the companies from which you order the goods for sale:

- Acting humanely
- Living by commendable values
- Treating others fairly and well (customers and employees alike)
- Ensuring a safe and healthy work environment
- Showing fiscal responsibility
- Contributing to society
- Protecting the environment

Here's an interesting example: Just today, we heard a radio news feature about Maytag Corporation—the home appliance giant—training returning U.S. soldiers from Iraq to launch new careers as appliance repair specialists, which have been in short supply. It's a win-win in the making—a great opportunity for the former enlisted men and women, a reliable workforce, and excellent public relations for Maytag. And surely, it will prompt someone next week or next month, who heard the same news feature, to pass up other brands and buy a Maytag washer or dryer in appreciation of the company's unique recruitment efforts.

On the other hand, it is not uncommon to learn about people like one customer we know who switched long-distance phone service carriers after the company he had been using laid off 40,000 workers in a massive downsizing. He said, "I can't see giving my money to a company which finds people that expendable. They made my decision easier."

As another example, we know several people who, despite the incredible international success of Wal-Mart, refuse to set foot in their stores. Said one: "I lived in Texas when Wal-Mart first started opening its huge stores in small towns there. I saw what that did to the local economies, devastating the mom-and-pop, Main Street businesses. I haven't spent a dime in a Wal-Mart, and I never will."

Are these customers "Lone Rangers"? Or are they among the growing number of passionate and informed consumers who refuse to support companies that act in ways inconsistent with their own ideals and sense of fair play? Half an hour on the Internet will unearth plenty of information about the newest financial trend, Socially Responsible Investing (SRI). There are apparently plenty of people who won't put money into mutual funds if any of the companies in the fund manufacture harmful chemicals or sell tobacco products, for example, and dozens of watchdog Web sites for companies that track environmental concerns, political ties, and other big-business red flags—Oligopoly Watch, the Domini 400 Social Index, and Corporate Accountability International, to name a few. In some facets of retail, labor unions also serve as watchdogs, looking out for their member workers and interpreting "citizenship" to include fair hiring practices, competitive wages, and safe working conditions.

Nobody said corporate citizenship wasn't controversial, either. Consider for a moment the food vendors that are now scrambling to adapt their product lines to help combat obesity . . . the workplaces that ban smoking, angering the workers who have no intention of quitting . . . the myriad decisions not to sell products made with sweatshop labor, or packaging that is not biodegradable, or cosmetics with ingredients that have been tested on animals. Trying to do the right thing can become a very complicated matter.

For every consumer poll, there is also a corporate executive poll about the hot topics of values and citizenship. A 2003–2004 survey by the Center for Corporate Citizenship at Boston College, with the U.S. Chamber of Commerce and the Hitachi Foundation, found companies at different stages in their citizenship commitments. About 10 percent are doing nothing beyond basic compliance with laws and industry standards; another 10 percent are widely known for their social and environmental activism. Companies like Ben & Jerry's, Land's End, Patagonia, and Timberland have made these values central to their consumer appeal as well as their mission statements. Most companies fall somewhere between the two extremes.[8]

Most retailers are deluged with requests from nonprofit groups, asking for everything from donated merchandise for the ubiquitous "silent auction" to big-money sponsorships of major events in a community. When cash is in short supply, an alterative that impacts internal morale as much as the company's public image is time—by allowing employees to volunteer for charitable causes, at least partly on the company's watch. Like any other large-scale project, this type of philanthropy works best when it is supported with a company-run structure that is created to set community outreach goals and budgets, take requests, review them regularly with the goals in mind, match interested workers to appropriate causes, and so on.

Whether it's a workplace or a charitable effort, no one gets excited about being average. Corporate citizenship doesn't mean that every department store has to get out there and clothe all homeless people in a three-county area. There are plenty of less ambitious causes that can still make employees proud to be working for the organization. The measure of a worthwhile cause is not how lofty it sounds to an outsider, or how it assuages the social conscience, or how much media coverage it can generate in a fiscal year. A good cause is one that makes sense to employees, deepening their commitment and adding meaning to their work—because the work they are asked to do is worthy of their best effort.

## CHAPTER SUMMARY

While the retail industry isn't at the "bottom of the barrel" when it comes to ethical concerns and living by well-defined standards of conduct, this chapter proves that there is room for improvement and offers numerous suggestions, both for companies and individuals. Most companies have a written set of values, ethics, and/or a code of conduct, but the usefulness of these documents lies in the follow-through in all levels of the organization.

Some stumbling blocks to successful follow-through were mentioned in the chapter, including employees' tendency to not tell managers the "whole truth" about unpleasant situations or, worse, to say nothing at all rather than impart bad news. Steps were given to rethink even the most mundane entry-level positions to make them more interesting and meaningful, which prompts greater personal accountability on the part of the worker.

In retail, core values extend to the way people deal with customers as well as coworkers; customers assume the way companies treat their workers is the way they will be treated as well. This, and the increased social and environmental concerns of many people, make it all the more important to be known as a company with a conscience. Customers expect generosity when it comes to charitable endeavors and employee volunteer opportunities, and vigilance in fiscal management and prudent use of natural resources. For the retailer who can juggle it all, the rewards of community concern and a true corporate conscience extend far beyond monthly sales figures. They can help galvanize a workforce, giving them a shared sense of identity and purpose.

## DISCUSSION QUESTIONS

1. What do you think it takes to be a good role model as a retail manager? How would you model good character to a workforce of entry-level employees?
2. The section on "Getting to the Core" contains a few examples of companies not "practicing what they preach." Pick three of them and explain (in one or two paragraphs each) why you believe these things happen.
3. How are the core values in a retail business different than in other types of companies, where employees don't deal directly with the public?
4. Do you make decisions about products or investments based on any particular social convictions? If so, explain them. If not, why not?
5. The chapter discussed charitable causes and social issues, but what about political donations, lobbying, and the like? How should these be included in a company's ethics and values? What if the company president is a die-hard member of one political party?

## ENDNOTES

1. *The 1999 National Business Ethics Study,* Walker Information, Indianapolis, Indiana, ©Walker Information, 1999.
2. See endnote 1.
3. See endnote 1.
4. Dr. Leonard L. Berry, "The Substance of Success," *Retailing Issues Letter,* Andersen and the Center for Retailing Studies, Texas A&M University, College Station, Texas, July 2001.
5. See endnote 4.
6. Bob Davies, "Integrity in Business: The Secret to Increased Sales," *Retailer News Online,* www.retailernews.com, October 2001.

7. Ian Wilhelm, "Poll Finds Public Supports Corporate Giving," *Chronicle of Philanthropy*, Washington, D.C., January 20, 2005. ©Chronicle of Philanthropy, property of Chronicle of Higher Education.
8. Philip Mirvis and Bradley Googins, "The Best of the Good," *Harvard Business Review*, December 2004.

# MANAGING IN DIFFICULT SITUATIONS

Retail management today is an extremely complex career field, and it requires skills and knowledge that go far beyond tracking sales, managing inventories, and supervising employees. In other chapters, we've detailed some of the federal employment laws with which managers must be familiar, as well as outlined the basic structure and functions of unions and employee benefit plans. You've also learned how to hire and retain good employees, and how to earn their loyalty by setting and sticking to ethics and values on behalf of your company.

However, sometimes issues crop up that, at first glance, seem to be beyond the scope of a typical manager's duties. We've lumped them into the category of potentially difficult situations that managers must face realistically in today's workplace. These include

- Drug abuse, prevention, and impairment testing
- Off-the-clock work
- Smokers and smoke-free workplaces
- Workplace violence
- Defusing coworker conflicts

In short, managers every day confront myriad other factors that seem to have little to do with selling products—but all are critical issues and must be dealt with professionally nonetheless.

## DRUG ABUSE IN THE WORKPLACE

The Substance Abuse and Mental Health Services Association, part of the U.S. Department of Health and Human Services, estimates that nearly 8 percent of full-time workers ages 18 to 49 use illegal drugs.[1] As an employer or manager, part of your job is to ensure that these practices do not interfere with these workers' daily responsibilities, or anyone else's.

Most companies today have a written drug abuse policy, and many have chosen to enforce these policies by drug testing—to prescreen potential employees, after workplace accidents or other incidents that raise an individualized suspicion, and by companies with federal contracts. There have been repeated attempts by unions and individuals to have drug testing declared an unconstitutional invasion of privacy, but most federal court rulings have found testing to be a minimal intrusion that is outweighed by the safety of the workplace or the public in general.

There are exceptions, however. Government employees, and workers belonging to certain unions, have been largely exempted from drug testing precisely because it violates their Fourth Amendment rights, and/or their Fifth Amendment rights to "due process" in legal proceedings. Some states have also outlawed private-sector preemployment drug testing on similar grounds.

Companies that use drug testing are convinced it improves safety and productivity. But a number of studies have shown drug testing to be only somewhat effective in accomplishing these objectives. The reasons uncovered by the studies include

- Fatigue, illness, and prescription of over-the-counter medicines impact safety and productivity more than prohibited drug use.
- Most employees do not show up at the workplace acutely intoxicated, so the tests simply cannot detect drug use in a timely fashion, only a worker's drug use during the previous days or weeks.
- Drug testing can negatively impact morale, or prospective employees will find it offensive and not apply.
- Serious substance abusers find ways around the drug tests anyway.[2]
- The cost of testing is prohibitive, especially for small companies.

For these reasons and others, employee drug testing has declined gradually in the past decade. A 2000 American Management Association study of workplace surveillance and medical testing found that employee drug testing was at its lowest level in a decade, practiced by 81 percent of companies surveyed in 1996, but only 62 percent in 2004.[3]

If your company performs drug tests, its policy must meet all of the following guidelines, summarized from the Texas Workforce Commission report, "Drug Testing in the Workplace." Drug testing and its policies must be:

- **Clearly stated in writing.** Written drug-testing policies should state their purpose, how they are to be administered, what constitutes a violation, the personnel to which the policy applies, the consequences of violations, and the manner in which appeals are to be filed.
- **Administered in a fair, objective, and nondiscriminatory way.** Drug testing takes two primary forms: random and "for cause." Most employers who drug-test their employees use both. Once again, to avoid morale and litigation problems, companies must clearly state to their workers the circumstances under which they can be tested. For instance, random testing could be an annual or semiannual procedure, and for-cause testing could be triggered by reasonable suspicion based on a precisely defined list. A company may legally test some (but not all) employees, but only if it tests all workers in a specific category. Warehouse or dock workers, for example, could be subject to testing because their jobs involve safety issues, whereas clerical and sales personnel could be excluded. Companies with outside contracts may also have obligations to test those workers who have contact with the contracting company. Whatever the specific situation, the best way

to minimize misunderstanding and potential legal challenges is to establish and enforce the policy in a fair and easily understandable way.

- **Clearly defined and nonpunitive.** Also important are clearly defined parameters for what represents a "failed" test. Many legal medications create "false positives" on initial drug tests, and there are also levels of certain substances such as alcohol or prescription medications that are considered to be acceptable. Whatever the company policy might be in this area, it must be clear and understandable to every worker affected by testing.
- **Absolutely confidential.** Improper release of employee drug test results can result in serious and expensive legal consequences—regardless of the outcome of the tests.[4]

## EXAMPLE OF A DRUG-TESTING POLICY

Here's an example of a workplace drug-testing policy, created by the Texas Workforce Commission as a template for state businesses:

DRUG-FREE WORKPLACE POLICY

It is the purpose of XYZ Corporation, Inc. (the Company) to help provide a safe and drug-free work environment for our clients and our employees. With this goal in mind and be-cause of the serious drug abuse problem in today's workplace, we are establishing the following policy for existing and future employees of XYZ Corporation, Inc.

The Company explicitly prohibits:

The use, possession, solicitation for, or sale of narcotics or other illegal drugs, alcohol, or prescription medication without a prescription on Company or customer premises or while performing an assignment.

Being impaired or under the influence of legal or illegal drugs or alcohol away from the Company or customer premises, if such impairment or influence adversely affects the employee's work performance, the safety of the employee or of others, or puts at risk the Company's reputation.

Possession, use, solicitation for, or sale of legal or illegal drugs or alcohol away from the Company or customer premises, if such activity or involvement adversely affects the employee's work performance, the safety of the employee or of others, or puts at risk the Company's reputation.

Continued

The presence of any detectable amount of prohibited substances in the employee's system while at work, while on the premises of the company or its customers, or while on company business. "Prohibited substances" include illegal drugs, alcohol, or prescription drugs not taken in accordance with a prescription given to the employee.

The Company will conduct drug testing under any of the following circumstances:

RANDOM TESTING: Employees may be selected at random for drug testing at any interval determined by the Company.

FOR-CAUSE TESTING: The Company may ask an employee to submit to a drug test at any time it feels that the employee may be under the influence of drugs or alcohol, including, but not limited to, the following circumstances: evidence of drugs or alcohol on or about the employee's person or in the employee's vicinity, unusual conduct on the employee's part that suggests impairment or influence of drugs or alcohol, negative performance patterns, or excessive and unexplained absenteeism or tardiness.

POST-ACCIDENT TESTING: Any employee involved in an on-the-job accident or injury under circumstances that suggest possible use or influence of drugs or alcohol in the accident or injury event may be asked to submit to a drug and/or alcohol test. "Involved in an on-the-job accident or injury" means not only the one who was injured, but also any employee who potentially contributed to the accident or injury event in any way.

If an employee is tested for drugs or alcohol outside of the employment context and the results indicate a violation of this policy, the employee may be subject to appropriate disciplinary action, up to and possibly including discharge from employment. In such a case, the employee will be given an opportunity to explain the circumstances prior to any final employment action becoming effective.

*Source:* Texas Workforce Commission, Austin, Texas.

## Impairment Testing

"Traditional" drug testing does not and cannot detect whether an employee is tired, stressed out, emotionally upset, or debilitated by illness or associated medicines to the point that he or she cannot safely do their job. So the newest trend in this field is known as impairment testing (IT) or "fit-for-duty" testing. Like drug testing, the aims are safety and productivity. But unlike drug testing, which measures past behavior, IT measures up-to-the-moment ability to work, against an employee's initially established "baseline performance." These tests vary in type, technique, and technology, but generally they measure for

- Spatial orientation
- Visual acuity
- Reaction time
- Hand-eye coordination
- Decision-making/executive function

More important, impairment testing does not test for *drugs* per se; it tests for *impairment*, regardless of the source. Most IT systems are sensitive to impairment created by drugs (illegal, prescription, and over-the-counter), alcohol, sleep deprivation, emotional or physical stress, and combinations of all of them.

Very few companies currently use IT, primarily because there are few providers of such systems. The main reason certain companies do use IT is that they face serious safety problems if employees come to work impaired—and they are aware that drug testing is not especially effective in actually measuring the ability of workers to perform their jobs safely.[5]

A National Workrights Institute study of 18 companies using IT found that all of them felt their choice to be successful: 87 percent called it superior to urine testing, and 82 percent said it improved workplace safety. In addition, the companies reported that 90 percent of their employees accepted impairment testing.[6] One reason for the wider acceptance is that most people realize human error is the cause of most workplace accidents, and acknowledge that people err less when they are alert.

An example of an IT system is the "Bowles-Langley Alertness Test," a small, computerized unit that can be mounted on a wall. Workers insert their individual "smart cards" to activate it, and the unit displays 30 to 40 screens designed to test a worker's readiness for work. It can be adapted to test for different work skills and takes about one minute per test. When the test is over, the machine compares the results to the worker's smart card baseline.[7]

A side benefit of IT is that it is a learning tool, of sorts, as well as a worker surveillance system. Employees can learn by results whether they need to increase their sleep, reduce their partying, or change the way they medicate themselves when they're ill. Downsides to impairment testing include workers' uneasiness about "constant" testing or surveillance, bottlenecks during shift changes, and the difficulty of setting impairment thresholds that determine when workers can still work at safety-critical jobs, when they need to be given less demanding work, and/or when they need to be sent home.

# OFF-THE-CLOCK WORK

Off-the-clock work is the practice of asking, demanding, or requiring hourly workers to start work before they "clock in" or keep working after they "clock out." A classic example is related in this excerpt from a November 2004 *New York Times* article:

> "I'd be clocking out, and (the assistant manager would) point out all this stuff, saying, 'This isn't done, and if you leave before this is done, you won't have a job Monday morning,' " said (Aaron) Payne, an Army veteran who served in Iraq. "It happened almost every night. I'd usually have to stay one and a half or two extra hours."[8]

The consequences of these actions (in this case, the employer was Wal-Mart) are lawsuits in dozens of states and several big-dollar payouts: The retail giant settled for $50 million in a 2000 suit involving 69,000 Colorado workers; a 2002 Oregon case also went against the company, but the back-pay penalty covered only 83 workers. Since then, Wal-Mart has changed company policies and procedures: Cashiers can no longer ring up customers if they are not on the clock, new employees are told not to work off-the-clock, and managers are told in writing to neither require nor allow such work.

The practice remains widespread, however, and in 2003 and 2004, the Department of Labor filed suits against numerous companies in several different industries, demanding compliance with federal regulations that prohibit the practice, and getting back pay for the affected employees. In November 2003, for example, the Labor Department secured a $4.8 million settlement with T-Mobile; in February 2004, it won $180,000 from the Hanna Steel Corporation for 500+ employees; in April 2004, it ordered the Pleasantview Healthcare Center in Tennessee to pay $44,887 to 41 employees.

In every case, the department found that employees were forced under threat of dismissal or promise of advancement to start working before they clocked in or continue working after they clocked out. In the Hanna case, it was "only" five minutes, but that five minutes added up to a $180,000 judgment against the company—and a loss of goodwill among its employees.[9]

United Parcel Service found out about this the hard way, too. The company routinely deducted payment for one-hour lunch breaks employees rarely took anyway in order to keep up with UPS productivity goals. A disgruntled Washington State driver filed a lawsuit on behalf of all state UPS drivers—and won $12 million in back pay for herself and them. Four years later, Illinois UPS drivers filed a similar lawsuit and, four years after that, won $7.25 million in damages.[10]

The bottom line on off-the-clock work: Don't do it. Don't require it of workers under your supervision, and don't passively allow it to happen around you—even if your bonuses and compensation are tied to cost cutting that off-the-clock work can help achieve.

Not only is off-the-clock fundamentally unfair to your staff and likely to reduce morale, there are a host of federal and state laws prohibiting it. These laws favor employees by stipulating that companies are obligated to stop work for which they don't want to pay. A company cannot defend itself by saying employees agreed or volunteered to do it, or that they hid their off-the-clock work from management.

In addition, as might be expected, most companies will deny that they have an off-the-clock policy or authorized any of their managers to use the practice. In other words, if your company gets sued for requiring/demanding/allowing off-the-clock work, the executives don't take the fall; the managers do. This idea is echoed by Steve Drapkin, an attorney for the Employers Group, a nonprofit association that provides human resources support for more than 5,000 companies.

> In most cases, the allegations you hear about involve individual managers who are acting to enhance the profitability of their own units, rather than reflecting any company-wide practices or policies.[11]

As with drug testing and other personnel policies that can be misunderstood, misinterpreted, or misapplied, there are several steps a company can take to protect itself (and its management team) from off-the-clock legal claims:

- Have written polices that make it clear to management and workers alike what counts as on-the-clock work time, that employees report and document their hours worked accurately, and that managers ensure their workers are not working off the clock. These policies need to be disseminated and understood during new employee and new manager orientation.
- Require managers and employees to review and sign off on the accuracy of employee time sheets. That way, potential off-the-clock claims can be countered with the document, which becomes evidence that the employee deliberately worked off the clock, then misrepresented his or her true hours when signing the time sheet certification.
- Ensure that automatic timekeeping systems are accurate and properly track not only basic hours but overtime, shift differentials, and other forms of premium pay.

Finally, regular reminders about proper time sheet and payroll procedures should be as important to a company as sales and productivity meetings. It's some of the best insurance companies can have against both "rogue" managers and illegitimate off-the-clock work claims.[12]

## THE SMOKE-FREE WORKPLACE

The retail industry has been sharply divided over the idea of banning smoking in retail businesses. At issue is the health of employees and customers, versus the rights of business owners to permit smoking on their own premises if they wish. The restaurant industry has been especially vocal—and also sharply divided—since smoking after mealtimes was an accepted custom for decades. But today, only about 22 percent of Americans smoke, which means 78 percent of them do not.[13]

Tobacco companies, well aware of the loss of income they suffer when smoking bans are enacted, have suggested alternatives to make indoor smoking more palatable: courtesy, accommodation, and better ventilation systems. However, health experts counter that only the smoky odor is dissipated by ventilation—the deadly chemicals in secondhand tobacco smoke remain airborne, to settle on surfaces and build up over time. Increasingly, smoking is being seen as a public health issue rather than an annoying habit. So at this writing (and the number changes every year as state legislatures debate the topic), a dozen states and about 100 cities or counties have passed some type of no-smoking ("Clean Indoor Air") legislation. In 2004, 11 states also increased their cigarette taxes.[14]

Most retailers see the handwriting on the wall, so to speak. They have already restricted workplace smoking in response to customers' requests, for fire safety reasons, to keep the store cleaner, and to protect the quality of the merchandise for sale. Some merchants receive small discounts on their health and/or liability insurance coverage for going smoke-free. Employees who continue to light up are seen outdoors, puffing away on their "smoke breaks," no matter what the weather. Some are okay with it; others feel ostracized.

In individual workplaces, it usually falls on supervisors to remedy specific complaints. If work breaks are given, they should be given equally to smokers and nonsmokers. If a store does not have a written tobacco-use policy, a group of employees that represents every department in the organization should be recruited to do the research and work together to create one. "Research" includes looking at the store's current demographics; percentage of smokers; how the issue has been dealt with thus far; the cost and availability of local "quit programs" and other resources; and the health, legal, and economic aspects for this particular business or location. Is there suitable outdoor space for smokers? What about workers who decide to chew tobacco instead of smoke? What should the policy reflect about image of the store?

When it is enacted, the policy should be enforced in the same way as any other health and safety policy. Going smoke-free is not as simple as putting up a few signs and moving the ashtrays from the employee break room to the outdoors. An effective written policy includes the following terms:

- A rationale for the policy—explain why it's being done
- A timeline for implementation of the policy
- A phase-in period, with specific smoking restrictions during this period
- An education component to provide information about the policy and how it will be introduced to new employees in the future
- Assistance, support groups, and/or incentives for smokers who would like to quit, often company-paid
- Clear wording of the policy for signage, job postings, and so on
- Specifics for enforcement, with penalties for noncompliance[15]

The controversy is expected to continue about tobacco use on the job. Some companies are openly refusing to hire smokers in an attempt to lower health care costs, citing smokers' increased health problems, accident rates, and absences compared to nonsmokers. But at least 28 states have laws that say workers who smoke cannot be discriminated against.[16]

## WORKPLACE VIOLENCE

There are no specific state or federal laws dealing with workplace violence, but it has been a growing area of concern during the last two decades as shooting incidents have proliferated around the country, impacting businesses and organizations as different as post offices, manufacturing plants, and law offices.

An average of 20 workers are murdered on the job every week in the United States; another 1 million are assaulted on the job annually in U.S. workplaces. The very nature of retail business makes it at least somewhat riskier than other industries in terms of violent crime. According to the National Institute for Occupational Safety and Health (NIOSH), factors that increase the risk for workplace violence include

- Contact with the public
- Exchange of money
- Working alone or in small numbers
- Working late-night or early-morning hours
- Working in high-crime areas
- Guarding valuable property or possessions
- Working in community-based settings[17]

As you can see, many retailers face multiple risk factors. The most recent federal workplace crime–related figures were compiled by the Occupational Safety and Health Administration (OSHA) in 1996, but they showed the highest annual homicide risks in the following types of retail establishments.[18]

- Liquor stores (7.5 deaths per 100,000 workers)
- Gas stations (4.8)
- Jewelry stores (4.7)
- Grocery and convenience stores (3.8)
- Restaurants and bars (1.5)

In addition, OSHA listed the retail *job types* that showed the highest risk of on-the-job death or assault:

- Gas station and garage employees (5.9 deaths per 100,000 workers)
- Stock handlers and baggers (3.5)
- Sales supervisors, store owners (3.3)
- Cashiers, salesclerks (3.1)

In response to these figures, OSHA began encouraging employers to develop written workplace violence prevention policies, and has suggested several key components of such policies:

**Management commitment.** OSHA cites this as an "essential precondition" to the success of a workplace violence prevention policy. The policy must state plainly that there is "zero tolerance" for verbal and non-verbal threats and related actions, and that managers will take all threatening and violent incidents seriously by investigating them and taking corrective action. The policy must also assign responsibility and authority to managers and employees "with appropriate training and skills," and hold them accountable for their performance.

**Reporting procedures.** There must be a system in place to promptly report, document, and track incidents that occur "in and near" the establishment, and safeguards built into the system so that anyone who reports a problem is not punished or discriminated against for speaking up.

**Employee involvement.** Workplace risk reduction is a group effort, and people should be encouraged to make suggestions, train new employees, perform routine security inspections, share their own experiences to benefit the group, and the like. Their vigilance may also recognize and defuse a potentially volatile situation with a coworker.

**Public involvement.** Landlords and fellow building tenants, the local police, insurance providers, and neighbors should all be part of the process. Some retailers hire outside consultants to provide training and make security recommendations.

**Hazard analysis.** A number of studies—including interviews with convicted robbers—have pinpointed what makes stores more "attractive" as targets: large amounts of cash on hand, an obstructed view of the counters; a low risk of recognition (lack of security cameras, poor visibility from outside the store, the relative isolation of the building or low foot traffic at certain times of day), and easy access and escape routes. A worksite hazard analysis with these factors in mind, and periodic reassessments, should be part of the written plan.

An excellent starting point is to look at the records of the business for the past two or three years, to see what types of incidents have occurred in the neighborhood as well as at the store location, and what types of employee disciplinary actions have been taken.[19]

Many companies now have written policies prohibiting weapons of various types in the workplace, or even in the vehicles of employees parked in company lots. This can raise Second and Fourth Amendment issues about searches and seizures and the right to bear arms, but the courts—as they have with First Amendment issues in the workplace—have usually upheld the rights of employers to run their businesses as they see fit.

Obviously, the best way to minimize the chances of workplace violence is to ensure that managers treat all employees as fairly as possible, that training is offered to recognize and mitigate tense situations, and that effective and accessible grievance procedures exist so that frustrated or angry employees have an acceptable way to resolve problems.

## Defusing Coworker Conflict

It is true that most retail-related workplace violence involves robbery. But among coworkers, the seeds of personality conflict are often sown long before a violent incident or even a tense verbal exchange. From

2002 to 2004, for example, of the 88 fatal incidents of workplace violence (in which 144 people were killed and 98 wounded):

- 43.6 percent were committed by current employees
- 22.5 percent were committed by former employees
- 21.4 percent were acts of domestic violence that happened on the job
- 12.5 percent were committed by clients or customers of the business[20]

Could these have been prevented? By and large, the experts say yes—with formal instruction on basic threat assessment, the identification of warning signs, and methods to defuse employee hostility.

Most coworker conflicts are certainly not life-or-death situations, but they can make life most unpleasant for the employees involved, and others on the same shift or sales floor. And they end up in the manager's purview, sooner or later. What to do?

Many such concerns begin with the so-called "difficult" employee. Others cannot help but notice when one person clearly isn't playing by the same rules—consistently showing up late or taking long lunch breaks, spending hours on personal calls, treating customers rudely, or simply performing at a lower level than his or her coworkers. It is estimated that

## STAYING IN CONTROL

**10 TIPS FOR MANAGING DIFFICULT EMPLOYEES**

1. Make clear what is expected from them.

2. Set deadlines.

3. Outline consequences.

4. Hold them accountable.

5. Have a peer hold them accountable.

6. Communicate often, and immediately when something is wrong.

7. Criticize softly and behind closed doors.

8. When they do something well, praise them in front of others.

9. Remember, they are people first and employees second. Try to understand why they keep making mistakes.

10. Don't let them drag down high-performing employees.

*Source:* Dana Knight, "Difficult Workers," *The Indianapolis Star*, Indianapolis, Indiana. Reprinted in *The Idaho Statesman*, Boise, Idaho, March 13, 2005.

about 10 percent of all employees fall into this category, either chronically difficult or low-performing. This is the person who always has an excuse for doing less, or doing it differently, than what is expected of him or her.[21]

As corporate coach and mentor Nicholas Nigro puts it, negative feedback does not have to be delivered in a negative fashion. Being sensitive and perceptive as you deliver expectations and consequences is the mark of a good manager. If feedback is regular, instead of only when someone screws up, and delivered in a straightforward, matter-of-fact tone instead of with anger or sarcasm, it will be easier to deliver bad news as well as good.

In *The Everything Coaching and Mentoring Book,* Nigro suggests the following multistep approach to a specific conflict between two employees that is impacting their job performance.[22] He calls the feuding coworkers "Frank" and "Dawn."

- Call Frank in and talk to him. Tell him precisely what's expected of him as an employee with a specific job to do and performance goals to be met. Ask him what he thinks the solutions to his performance problems are and what ideas he has to improve his working relationship with Dawn. Then, follow the same course with Dawn.
- Once you've spoken your piece and carefully listened to your two quarreling staff members on an individual basis, your next move is to call Frank into your office for round two, and tell him some of Dawn's ideas for forging a better working relationship. You need to gauge his reactions to her suggestions. Then, bring Dawn in (separately), and tell her some of Frank's ideas for rectifying their mutually destructive performances.
- Round two is indispensable, because round three involves you refereeing Frank and Dawn in the same room, and tying together all that you've learned in your one-on-one discussions with them. You've heard their sides of the story; you've gotten their reactions to what each had to say about the other's suggestions about righting things; and now you, Frank, and Dawn are all coming together to agree upon solutions for a positive outcome to a problem.

"Traditional managers," says Nigro, "are apt to skip rounds one and two of this process and call in their battling employees right from the start, telling them point-blank, 'Work it out between yourselves . . . or else!' Sure, in the end, the battling employees themselves will have to work out their differences, or nothing positive will happen. That much is certain. But you have a much better chance of securing positive outcomes if you talk with each employee individually, gather what information you can as to the causes of the personal or work-related problems leading to the diminished performances, and then proceed from there. . . . Round three, then, is as productive as possible because you did your homework."[23]

Nigro stresses that the outcome of mediating coworker conflicts is not to make them the best of friends—it's to secure positive results in their on-the-job performance. Yes, it is time-consuming, but so is unproductive sniping by coworkers, at each other and the rest of the team.

## CHAPTER SUMMARY

This chapter covered several of the toughest situations managers face, and should prove that, in almost all cases, they can be dealt with most effectively if the retailer has a written policy about the topic before problems arise. These policies must be clearly communicated, easy to understand, administered fairly, and regularly scrutinized for updates if necessary. For example, guidelines and a sample policy for drug testing employees were included, along with a discussion of impairment testing as the latest trend in this somewhat controversial field.

Off-the-clock work is another difficult challenge, balancing employers' expectations for work that must be done with employees' rights to be paid when they are on the job. The chapter mentioned several lawsuits against employers for requiring employees to stay beyond their normal work shifts without paying them for overtime.

The rights of both smokers and nonsmokers come into play with today's awareness of the dangers of secondhand smoke. If your city, county, or state does not already have a Clean Indoor Air law, taking a company stand on where and when employees can smoke on the job, or making the store smoke-free, should be done in writing. The decision is ideally made with the input of employees, along with research into the health, legal, and economic impact of both smoking and nonsmoking choices. Both groups have rights on which court challenges can be made.

Retail businesses have slightly increased threats of workplace violence simply because they are open to the public, and the chapter outlined steps for an effective violence prevention policy. The chapter ended with methods for dealing with so-called "difficult" workers and coworker conflicts, to help prevent escalating tension that arises from time to time on the job.

## DISCUSSION QUESTIONS

1. What are the key elements of a company drug-testing policy?
2. What are the pros and cons of impairment testing versus drug testing? Which system do you think would be more appropriate for a small retail workplace? For a large one?
3. Why is off-the-clock work unacceptable? How can managers reduce the incidence of deliberate or inadvertent off-the-clock work?
4. What kinds of skills should be included in retail workplace violence prevention training? What would you find most helpful?
5. Have you ever been part of, or witnessed, a coworker conflict on the job? Describe it and how the employer or manager handled it. Knowing what you know now, how would you have done it differently had you been in charge?

## ENDNOTES

1. Dana Knight, "Is Employer Drug Screening on the Way Out?" *Indianapolis Star*. Reprinted in *The Idaho Statesman*, February 27, 2005.
2. "Workplace Testing: Medical Testing, Summary of Key Findings," American Management Association, New York, 2000.
3. See endnote 2.
4. "Drug Testing in the Workplace," Guidelines from the Texas Workforce Commission, Austin, Texas.
5. Debra Comer, "An Evaluation of Fitness-for-Duty Testing: Part I," presented at the 103rd Annual Convention of the American Psychological Association, New York, August 15, 1995.
6. "Impairment Testing: Does It Work?" National Workrights Institute, Princeton, New Jersey (undated material).
7. Bowles-Langley Technology, Inc., Alameda, California, March 2005.
8. Steven Greenhouse, "Lawsuits and Change at Wal-Mart," *New York Times*, November 19, 2004.
9. See endnote 8.
10. David N. Mark, "Off-the-Clock Work: What You Can Do about It," *Washington Free Press*, Seattle, Washington (undated material).
11. See endnote 10.
12. Paul L. Siegel, "Developing a 'Clockwork' State of Mind: Avoid 'Off-the-Clock' Work Claims by Non-Exempt Employees," International Risk Management Institute, Dallas, Texas, February 2005. Reproduced with permission of the publisher. Further reproduction prohibited. (Visit www.irmi.com for free, practical, and reliable risk and insurance information.)
13. National Center for Health Statistics, Centers for Disease Control, Hyattsville, Maryland, 2003.

14. Smoke Free World, Berkeley, California, March 2005.
15. "Introducing a Policy on Smoking in the Workplace," National Heart Foundation of Australia, Melbourne, Australia, 1995.
16. Kathy Barks Hoffman, "Smoke? Then You Won't Work at Some Companies," *Cincinnati Enquirer*, February 9, 2005.
17. "Risk Factors and Prevention Strategies," NIOSH, Washington, D.C., July 16, 1996.
18. "Recommendations for Workplace Violence Prevention Programs in Late-Night Retail Establishments," U.S. Department of Labor, OSHA, 1998.
19. See endnote 18.
20. Larry J, Chavez, Critical Incident Associates, "Workplace Violence—Can We Do More to Prevent It?" *Human Resource Executive* magazine, Horsham, Pennsylvania, October 2004.
21. Dana Knight, "Difficult Workers," *Indianapolis Star*, Indianapolis, Indiana. Reprinted in *The Idaho Statesman*, March 13, 2005.
22. Nicholas Nigro, *The Everything Coaching and Mentoring Book* (Avon, MA: Adams Media, an F & W Publishing Company, 2003).
23. See endnote 22.

# CUSTOMER
# SERVICE AND
# RELATIONSHIP
# BUILDING

Until now, this book has focused primarily on workplace laws, sound company policies, and positive employee-manager relationships. It's time to take a look at the reasons for abiding by the laws, writing the solid policies, and building the trusting relationships—they are all part of the effort to run an exemplary retail business that keeps customers coming back.

This chapter includes several important, consumer-focused topics:

- The emotions behind customer loyalty
- What customers mean by "service"
- Why customers leave
- Personalizing service to enhance loyalty
- Employees' commitment to service
- Questions to ask to gauge resistance to change

More and more retailers (and their suppliers) are coming to understand that the best way to grow business is by strengthening the relationships they already have rather than constantly looking for new ones. Not only have they finally learned that, in an era of tough competition and tight margins, losing old customers as quickly as they find new ones is too expensive, retailers have also realized that the cycle of "customers in/customers out" exacts other, more subtle costs. Without retained customers to pay the bills and keep profits and company spirits up, good employees are hard to find and keep. Aggressive pricing policies are difficult to implement, and long-term profit for owners' hard work and investment is almost impossible to come by.

It is not enough today to cut prices to attract buyers. Any retailer can do that, and the retail giants have proven that the rock-bottom bargain strategy has its merits. For other stores, the personal touch of building customer relationships is what will make the difference in building success.

However, customers can be fickle—and they have their own agendas. They are naturally suspicious of anyone who ardently requests their commitment. They are not easily impressed, and they know the difference between companies that genuinely care about them and those that try to manipulate them into thinking they do. In addition, technology has given customers the ability to become better educated and more sophisticated about their buying choices. This has resulted in a gradual shift in power from those who create or sell products and services to those who consume them. And frustrated by years of having to take whatever companies chose to "dish out," customers are making their feelings known by taking their business elsewhere when they are unhappy. Often, the retailer has no idea that they are gone. They don't complain—they simply don't come back.

# BUSINESS AS A HUMAN ENDEAVOR

At its heart, the retail business is a human endeavor where individuals meet, talk, work, and otherwise try to help and benefit one another. In Chapter 6, we discussed the importance of considering employees' emotions as well as their skills, and the rule can be applied to customers as well. Shopping itself is an intensely personal activity—people shop when they are happy, when they are sad, when they are stressed to the max and have needs that must be met promptly. It may be curtains for the new apartment, the perfect bridesmaids' dresses, or groceries in half an hour before picking the kids up at school. Emotions and satisfaction and loyalty are as much the currency of exchange today as dollars. It is fairly easy for retailers to ignore this fact, since emotions can be messy, fickle, and difficult to quantify.

Products are made better, faster, and smaller and are sold less expensively than ever before. But the transaction itself must be sufficiently satisfying on a human level to keep customers coming back to a store and recommending it to their friends. Customizing a product is not the same as personalizing it. Loyalty cannot be measured solely by purchase frequency. It is an emotional response that represents a person's level of comfort and trust with the store and the people who work there. So, in a world where customers have the power, as long as merchants continue to convey that they are really more interested in getting than giving—and more with creating an impression than actually caring about individual customers—gaining their loyalty will be impossible.

A 2004 survey of 241 retailers makes some revealing comparisons about what customers *really think* versus what merchants *assume* they think about "good customer service." (See Table 9-1.) Each group was asked to rank certain service-related factors in terms of their priority *to the customers*, not their importance to employees or their inclusion in store policies. The results show that customers and retailers' perceptions of "customer service" differ widely in some, but not all, cases.

## Why Customers Leave

Also in Chapter 6, we listed the major reasons employees leave their jobs in search of new ones. Now let's apply the same technique to customers. When the U.S Small Business Administration surveyed customers of a variety of retail merchants in 2004, the chief reason people cited for giving up on one store or business to buy from another is that

| Survey Statement | % of Customers Who Agree | % of Retailers Who Agree |
|---|---|---|
| It is extremely important that store employees be well educated about the merchandise. | 52 % | 61 % |
| It is extremely important that store employees get to know the customers. | 25% | 44% |
| It is extremely important that the merchandise offered be of high quality. | 20% | 35% |
| Customers are very concerned that prices on items are accurately marked. | 71% | 58% |
| It is extremely important that retailers do not share customers' information with other companies. | 73% | 59% |
| It is extremely important that stores be staffed with an adequate number of employees. | 47% | 31% |

**TABLE 9-1  2004 Survey Results**

*Source:* NRF Foundation/American Express 2004 Customer Service survey, the National Retail Foundation Federation, Washington, D.C.

the merchant's employees didn't seem to care about them, one way or the other. The "perception of noncaring" was mentioned by 68 percent of the survey respondents. Contrast this with the results in Table 9-1—only 25 percent of the customers in that survey felt it is "extremely important that store employees get to know customers." So it's obviously not about making friends. It's about just *being friendly*. Other reasons consumers gave for leaving a retailer included the following:

Dissatisfaction with a product        14 percent
Dissatisfaction with prices        9 percent
Taking a friend's recommendation        5 percent
Moving away from the area        3 percent
Death of the customer        1 percent

Apart from the last two, a good merchant ought to be asking some serious questions about how to better serve customers with courtesy and common sense.[1]

Why is it important to ask? Perhaps because, between 2000 and 2003, consumer complaints about retail stores to Better Business Bureau locations nationwide increased 104 percent.[2] Retailers everywhere should be asking, "Why?"

## Customer Efficiency

So what do customers want, and how do retailers go about giving it to them? Major retail consulting firms like McMillan|Doolittle of Chicago believe it is time to rethink the concepts of productivity and efficiency. They explain that retailers are quick to try things that will make them more productive and efficient—new point-of-sale systems, just-in-time logistics for restocking, and so on—but they haven't focused on the things that will make *their customers* more productive and efficient in the store.

With everyone strapped for time, efficiency has become a huge loyalty proposition. McMillan|Doolittle cites a survey that says 64 percent of consumers will leave the store if they think it's going to take too long to check out, and 70 percent say they won't shop at all at a store where the retailer "wastes their time." Shoppers want convenience and speed, and the company suggests giving it to them by tending to the "Five Cs" of consumer efficiency:

- **Clarity.** Maintaining a clear focus on what you offer and stand for, and communicating that day in and day out through consistent execution, helps consumers decide where to shop and makes it easier for them to find what they need. If a retailer's positioning is not clearly defined and communicated, the store will likely be confusing to consumers. Great examples of clarity of focus are the Gap's multiple formats, and the Container Store.
- **Choice.** Stores are getting bigger, but not necessarily more productive for customers. The old belief that retailers are buying agents for their customers holds true in the customer efficiency frontier. Both too much choice and too little choice waste customers' time. Choice, "edited" to be just right for the target audience, wins big. Kohl's is a great example of a retailer with an assortment tailored efficiently for its target audience.
- **Control.** Customers want to be in control of their shopping experience. They are comfortable with gathering information and shopping on their own. They do not like pushy salespeople, processes that are not flexible enough to handle different shopping situations, and store layouts that waste their time. Most retailers do not have a clue how to approach this key element in the customer efficiency equation.

- **Communications.** Deciding what information to provide customers, as well as where, when, and how to provide it, are critically important to improving customer efficiency. Sometimes, salespeople need to provide the information. At other times, different methods (such as signage, point-of-sale brochures, phones, and increasingly the Internet) work best. Saturn and Target are role models in effective customer communication.
- **Checkout.** Nothing wastes customers' perceived (or real) time more than inefficient handling at the checkout. Whatever the problem is— poorly managed checkout lanes, inoperative equipment, or failure to take exceptions offline—most retailers don't pay nearly enough attention to this last "moment of truth" with customers.[3]

## Repeat Buying vs. Loyalty

The other key finding of marketing researchers is that loyalty—to stores and to brands—cannot be accurately defined by a person's number of visits to stores and/or the "total spend" at the cash register, the types of details that retailers keep track of with customer loyalty cards or "frequent buyer" programs. As sales consultant Jim Barnes put it in an article to baby-product retailers:

> There is a tendency to confuse loyalty with retention—two concepts that are related, but certainly not the same thing. Retention is a behavioral concept; loyalty is not. A focus on retention creates a high-risk situation where a company may think its customers are a lot more loyal than they really are.[4]

Barnes points to the "natural human need to develop loyalties—not only to friends and family, but to organizations and to brands." Again, the emphasis is on emotion, not logic. But how is this accomplished? We know customers are short on time. Prompt and knowledgeable service goes a long way in terms of meeting their needs quickly, and it works as well in a "big-box" chain store as in a smaller, specialty store.

Retailers of all types can learn from the very specialized field of antique sales, where personalized service is as individual as the antiques themselves. These retailers must compete with big auction houses as well as a host of Internet sites for collectors' business. Their customers are not necessarily frequent purchasers, but they can be high-dollar customers. Experienced collectors are extremely knowledgeable and picky about the authenticity and condition of their merchandise. They are also the source of consignment merchandise for the retailers—so their loyalty is doubly valuable. In an article in *Maine Antique Digest*, writer David Vazdauskas found the successful antiques dealer is using service to reinforce customer loyalty, with tactics like these:

- From Erik Gronning of Vermont: "Scholarship is a way that I can differentiate myself. For every customer that walks into my shop, I'll spend as long as they want talking about or researching a single piece."
- From M. L. Coolidge of Northeast Auctions: "We actually call people back. Even if we don't think a certain consignment is for us, we'll refer them to the right place. Or if we see someone at a preview looking hesitantly at a desk, we'll encourage them to lift the lid and see what's inside."
- From Cathie DiGrazia of Massachusetts: "We try not to be pretentious. Instead of trying to *sell* to new customers, we try to assist them in the purchase process."

## ADDITIONAL "DOS" THAT CREATE RETAIL CUSTOMER LOYALTY

1. Do have beautiful and informative product displays and catalogs. Visually tempt customers with your merchandise, featuring exclusive or new items, and those that represent good values.

2. Do offer customers credit (and trust). Notwithstanding the risks of bad debt, no other retail factor engenders loyalty like a robust credit service. "Share of wallet" of credit customers can be more than three times that of cash customers.

3. Do offer customers a reliable shopping experience—a relevant range of items and prices with service to match it. "Reliable" in retail means you get what you need each time you visit the store.

4. Do stock and promote products for both the thrifty and the spendthrift customer. This keeps customers "choices" in your store instead of between several stores that offer similar products at different price points.

5. Do offer value for the money. No matter what the price of an item, it should be a fair balance between equity and price.

6. Do be a store that is both conveniently located and interesting to browse.

7. Do remove risk, by standing by your products with guarantees.

*Source:* Adapted from Bateleur Research Solutions, Johannesburg, South Africa. March 24, 2004.

- Harvey Pranian of Illinois holds an annual summer "yard sale" and also offers food and wine at a winter holiday open house, combining sales with social events that recognize loyal customers and instill camaraderie.

Antiques retailers have also discovered the value of the so-called "middle-market buyer," who may want to own some interesting pieces but most likely does not intend to become a serious collector. This person needs the seller's advice and opinions before making a purchase, and his or her loyalty is earned by providing a nonjudgmental introduction to the field. Vazdauskas says the smart retailer in this field "taps into deeper emotional needs" of the buyers—in this case, they are social interaction, self-fulfillment, entertainment, or "simply to amass or to covet."[5] In short, the underlying reason for the sale is as important as the sale itself.

## THE SERVICE-SAVVY EMPLOYEE

Do retail salespeople really think about the underlying reasons customers are standing in the juniors department—their excitement at picking out a prom dress, or their apprehension about trying on a swimsuit? Do they really *relate* to those feelings? As we all know, relationships involve and demand mutual effort, respect, and concern. There's no way to build lasting customer relationships without competent employees who are personally committed to entering into and nurturing these relationships, even when they may only last a few minutes at a time.

Achieving this level of commitment with employees requires a workforce in which each individual is as motivated to providing these relationships as individual customers are to enjoying their benefits. Learning to compete in a world where every offering must be personalized and unique requires that people in retail learn to think and act dramatically differently. Creating the fast, flexible, adaptive, friendly, customer-centric organization happens one sale at a time, and it is quickly becoming a prerequisite for survival in the future.

If the quality of service reflects the quality of management, here's an ominous statistic: In 2004, a Customer Experience Management (CEM) survey of 212 senior executives on four continents found that, despite their companies being "more committed to customer strategy" than they were three years ago, only 40.6 percent felt that their company *deserves* the loyalty of its customers. That's down from 55.5 percent in the previous year's survey.[6] Not all of them were retailers, but all sell products or services to someone as part of doing business.

Think about the loyal relationships *you* enjoy as a customer, and you will realize they have been built by employees who have the authority, the information, and the genuine desire to serve you—sometimes under extraordinary circumstances, when only exceptional service and personalized treatment will do. It is not gushing, fake friendliness, but skillful and pleasant assistance from dedicated employees that keeps you coming back again and again, no matter how special, cheap, or stiff the competition.

What can you do to ensure that these are the types of experiences customers have at your store? Building employees' commitment to good service is a multistep process:

**Make sure all employees have the authority to build a relationship.** In the same 2004 survey mentioned a moment ago, only 31 percent of the executives surveyed agree that their employees "have the tools and authority to actually serve the customers." That's a drop from 37 percent in 2003, and it signals that many companies either don't realize or don't capitalize on the critical nature of that one-on-one contact, no matter how brief, between employees and customers.[7]

Customers appreciate what your team can do, but they are also frustrated and/or turned off by whatever it is they can't or won't do. When this happens, the initial tendency is to blame the employee. But after further consideration, the customer usually ends up blaming the company. Give people the authority to do the right thing, whatever it may be. This is often as simple as allowing common sense to prevail.

For example, how many times have you gone shopping for a small appliance—a toaster oven, a tape recorder—seen the exact one you wanted on display, only to be told, "We're out of that item."

The knee-jerk (and commonsense) response: "What do you mean, you're out of that item? What about this one?"

"Oh, that's not for sale. That's only for display."

Common sense tells us that, if a customer wants this item, they should be able to purchase it—and perhaps at a discount if it's the display model. An employee who is allowed to exercise his or her own good judgment would be bagging the item and ringing up the sale by now.

And think about this for a moment: Why is the item being displayed at all if it is, indeed, out of stock? The store is asking for a disappointed customer and a difficult situation for the salesperson to resolve.

**Learn to trust the good judgment of your employees.** If you don't trust your employees to take the right and sensible course, why would they be the "point person" dealing with the customers in the first place?

A 2005 workplace productivity survey found that 79 percent of workers feel that they are, or have been, "micromanaged" on the job. Supervisors who feel they must try to control every facet of a department or project often do so because they underestimate the intelligence and the potential of their employees.[8]

Of course managers *are* allowed to worry that the people who work for them won't always use the best judgment. But the question then becomes, do you prevent anyone except the manager from making judgments at all? Or do you hire the best possible staff, train them to use their best judgment, and then give them the authority to do so?

**Allow people the chance to give all they want to give.** Losing customers' loyalty is not the only potential fallout from denying employees the authority to exercise their skill and judgment. As we all know from our own work experiences, if you're continually frustrated in your work and in your ability to do a good job because of people and policies that seem to prevent it, your dedication as an employee wanes and your commitment weakens. It's at that point that you tend to look elsewhere for satisfaction and reward—at another store.

**Have intelligent, knowledgeable, well-trained service people.** The retail transaction does not end with the sale. There are returns, exchanges, repairs, credit or billing questions, and special requests, which often require an even greater dose of common sense than the sale itself. No computer program, elaborate electronic help line, or e-mail message response system can take the place of a skilled cadre of knowledgeable employees empowered to listen to the customers and keep the relationships strong, especially when there's a problem. It still takes a human being to explain some processes, order missing instruction booklets, check on lost items ordered online, and think about whether "these pants or those" look better on the customer who emerges from the dressing room to seek an objective opinion.

And finally, all the empowerment and information in the world won't help if the spirit is missing. When it comes right down to it, don't you like doing business with people who seem to like doing business with you? When a retail sales clerk or a supermarket checkout person has a kind word, knows how to count out change correctly, and seems relatively pleased to be assisting us, the little bit of spirit and professionalism that they impart is infectious. They may not realize it at the moment, but the possibility of their store gaining our loyalty is greatly improved.

## "WHAT IF?" PLANNING FOR SERVICE PROBLEMS

Mistakes happen. Why not plan responses in advance? It would be unthinkable to enter a new fiscal year without a financial plan, or to attend a market without a buying plan. Addressing service problems without a plan can be just as negligent and costly. Employees can help by role-playing "what if . . . ?" scenarios at staff meetings and anticipating possible mistakes. Just thinking about what could go wrong makes people better prepared when things actually do go wrong. For less experienced workers, it helps build confidence and critical thinking skills.

What if the cash the customer gave me is counterfeit?

What if we're short-staffed?

What if the customer is angry, even after I've apologized?

What if the special order doesn't come in when I said it would?

What if it doesn't come in at all?

What if the POS terminal freezes up and I can't get it unstuck?

What if the software has a bug?

What if the toll-free customer support line is always busy?

## IDEAS, LARGE AND SMALL

In 2005, the Retail Industry Leaders Association (RILA) announced its members' top-priority projects for the year would be "enhancing the shopper experience and maximizing revenue from loyal customers." The association was compiling case studies from successful retail companies to share with members, including "actions that mimic the customer intimacy of 100 years ago, when sole-proprietor store owners knew neighborhood customers by name, knew which items would sell and which would not, extended credit to favored customers, and practiced micro-merchandising."[9]

In researching for this chapter, we've run across good ideas from a number of sources that illustrate a combination of modern-day business sense and old-fashioned service and morale-building. We'll share them here to prompt you to think of others.

- A men's clothing retailer deployed a database to store customers' measurements and made it available to every store. Sales are up because now women can buy clothing for the men in their lives that they know will fit.[10]

- One company provides textbook money for its sales interns who are attending high school and college.[11]
- One company has an intranet e-mail suggestion box for "Hassles"—anything that takes up more than a few minutes a day that is not part of a person's ordinary job. Employees take turns at acknowledging and then solving them, in teams of two, within one week of being reported.[12]
- One company has a daily 15-minute milk-and-cookies break to bring people from different departments together. Employees trade off serving and doing cleanup. In this company, they also share routine chores (sorting mail, watering plants, keeping office supplies stocked, cleaning the break room) once done by administrative assistants who had left the company. Instead of replacing them, their former salaries are used to buy the treats and put into "employee culture" and "community service" funds.[13]

## CHANGING THE SERVICE MIND-SET

What would stop a company from adopting any of those, or other good ideas? One of the biggest faults of retail organizations is that they can be slow to change. It is not that companies don't see changes coming—Sears surely saw Wal-Mart coming. IBM and Microsoft were at one time partners. American Airlines' and Southwest Airlines' headquarters are in the same city. United Parcel Service had any number of reasons why they didn't have to innovate faster to compete with upstart Federal Express, and Apple's failure to react fast enough to the Intel machine is legendary. In almost every case, where organizations have failed to react fast enough to maintain their leadership position, they have underestimated how quickly the value proposition was changing and how much they would have to fundamentally change to meet the challenges posed by new and different competitors.

It was not because these companies or their managers didn't work hard or were not committed to the effort, but because they figured they had plenty of time to react, plan, and strategize. Simply put, constancy was far more valued than adaptability.

Most efforts to change and quickly adapt are also hampered by the fact that there is natural resistance to substantial change. Organizations don't change—people change. This is why it is so important for managers to be able to inspire loyalty in their own workers, who then take ownership in and responsibility for their jobs, accept changes more readily, learn more quickly, and pass their natural enthusiasm along to the customers.

## Creating Change

Some interesting research for creating change can be found in the works of Carl Frost and Joseph Scanlon. A generation ago, they studied how to reinvent the nature of work—in this case, for factory workers. Herman Miller, Lincoln Electric, and Harley-Davidson are examples of companies that have adapted their teachings.

Before consultant Carl Frost would agree to work with a company, he would interview people at all levels. Frost called his questions, "A Quiz You Cannot Fail." Of course, if many of the employees did "fail" the test, Frost would not sign on to work with that company! What his quiz was really designed for was to gauge how well the organization could prepare for change. Here are the four questions he asked—and today, they are worth retailers' consideration when major changes are required in order to improve customer service levels:

- **Is there a compelling reason to change?** Frost believed that until people see their old behavior as unacceptable, they naturally resist change—especially if their past practices have proven to be successful.
- **Do you think you and your coworkers share a sense of how you would like things to be different?** He believed that if there were no unifying causes—if people couldn't agree on what to do or how to get started on it—it would be difficult to get them to commit to the effort without a better end in sight.
- **Do you believe significant, meaningful change is attainable in this company?** This question attempts to assess people's confidence level that the outcome would be worth the effort. After all, if they're resisting change, they won't think it can be attained.
- **Do you believe you will personally benefit from the anticipated changes?** The assumption here was that if the person believed that he or she *would not* benefit, or was uncertain about it, the person would be likely to resist the effort to change.

The theory seems like a blinding flash of the obvious. But it is amazing how rare it is for people in organizations to answer "yes" to each of these simple questions and to be able to discuss all the underlying issues they raise. It is more common for people to think they need to change, but not be clear as to exactly what to change or how to go about it.

Unfortunately, a shared sense of purpose is also rare. There may be company mission statements and vision statements, but a deeply held purpose that is the center of corporate identity and commitment is still too rare. Ask most people what they do for a living and they will give you their job title, job description, or specific skills. Rarely do they mention an important cause that unifies the efforts of the whole team, or explain why their job is fun and rewarding. In the process of creating change, there can be no commitment without asking the question: Commitment to what? If the answer is not a cause or goal that people feel is worthy of their sacrifice—and "a paycheck" doesn't count—they will resist and hold on to the status quo.

Confidence in the organization's ability to continuously renew is rare, too. Most people, especially in large organizations, are more cynical than confident—and understandably so. They have seen so many "flavor-of-the-month" training sessions and poorly implemented tools that they often look at any pronouncement of change and just roll their eyes.

And finally, people simply won't commit to changes that won't benefit them—even if they understand that the change benefits the bottom line. Here, Carl Frost's quiz is direct. Yet, most companies not only fail to ask the question but often pick methods that frustrate instead of providing opportunities for employees to get their personal needs satisfied. For instance, threatening an employee that he might lose his job or be laid off if he doesn't meet that sales quota will certainly change his behavior quickly! It will move him to do whatever is necessary to keep his job. Rarely is that about learning and motivation. Most often it means that the employee is being micromanaged, increasing his fear and inhibiting his ability to learn and adapt.

Again, the failure in attempting to build the fast, flexible, adaptive organization is not for lack of intelligence or effort. It most often is for lack of a common method and common set of assumptions about how to build such an organization and "fire up" (rather than fire) its employees. The truth is that most managers are much better at creating compliance than gaining commitment.

People don't resist change . . . they resist *being changed*. If this is true, then the manager's job is to educate and persuade, not manipulate and threaten. Freedom and choice are the foundations of commitment—and only with sincere commitment can an employee provide great customer service.

# CHAPTER SUMMARY

Customer loyalty involves more than the number of times customers visit a store or the amount of money they spend there. Much of this chapter focused on the emotional issues that surround loyalty, and the traits that trigger customers' emotions in retail situations. These include a convenient and efficient shopping experience, commonsense sales and return policies, and knowledgeable sales and service people with pleasant attitudes.

On the other hand, you also learned about the negative consequences of having uninformed or unempowered employees who don't appear to enjoy their jobs. Advice from several retail consultants in different countries was included, showing just how universal these traits are—both good and bad—and how they impact the overall shopping experience.

There were some discouraging figures quoted about how few managers and employees believe they are doing their best possible jobs or that they *deserve* their customers' loyalty. Then again, this information could be seen as an exciting opportunity for retailers to do things better. The chapter also included more than a dozen specific ways in which retail stores can become more customer-centric, using the example of the highly specialized antique business as a source of ideas, as well as other real-life examples from other types of merchants.

Today's customer expects store management to give sufficient training and authority to employees to be able to work with them, not only on sales but on after-sale needs such as repairs, exchanges, and getting answers to questions. In some cases, even the most sophisticated technology will never replace the human element of sales and service transactions.

The chapter ended by outlining the reasons that retail businesses, like so many others, have been slow to change. It detailed the work of Carl Frost and Joseph Scanlon in preparing companies for far-reaching change that will result in better customer service only if employees believe that the change will be personally meaningful, and if everyone in the company shares a similar goal or vision.

## DISCUSSION QUESTIONS

1. In your mind, what is the difference between customer retention and customer loyalty? Why is this difference important, as long as the customers keep coming back?
2. How can the sales tips in the section on antiques retailing be applied to other, more traditional types of stores?
3. What conclusions can you draw about the differences in percentages in Table 9-1 that would be useful to retailers in your community?
4. In a few paragraphs, describe one retail store (not a restaurant or bar) where you feel truly comfortable. Even if you don't like shopping very much overall, why do you enjoy shopping *there*? How are you treated—and why?
5. Think of your own idea, large or small, for making employees pay more attention to customer service. In this case, it cannot involve paying them bonuses or additional commissions—think more creatively! Can you think of ideas that wouldn't cost the company a dime but might still be effective motivators?

## ENDNOTES

1. Survey results, U.S. Small Business Administration, Washington, D.C., January 10, 2005.
2. Clayton Collins, "With Customers Griping, Retailers Finally Get the Message," *Christian Science Monitor*, January 31, 2005.
3. "Retailing's Next Frontier: The Efficient Consumer," *Retail Watch*, a publication of McMillan|Doolittle, Chicago, February 1999.
4. Jim Barnes, "From the Customer's Perspective: Defining Loyalty," *Baby Shop* magazine, Spring 2004.
5. David Vazdauskas, "Customer Loyalty: Where Competition and Economics Collide," *Maine Antique Digest*, March 2003.
6. "2004 Customer Experience Management (CEM) Global Survey," Strativity Group, Inc., Parsippany, New Jersey.
7. See endnote 4.
8. "2005 Workplace Productivity Survey," Society for Human Resource Management, Alexandria, Virginia.
9. Sandra L. Kennedy, president, Retail Industry Leaders Association, in *Chain Store Age* magazine, February 2005.
10. See endnote 9.
11. Leigh Buchanan, "Managing One-to-One," *Inc.* magazine, October 2001.
12. See endnote 11.
13. Ilan Mochari, "It's All in the Details," *Inc.* magazine, March 2002.

# RETAIL
# TECHNOLOGY
# AND TRENDS

The year 2005 began with the National Retail Federation's Annual Convention and Expo in January. The exhibit that received the most publicity was a mockup of a futuristic bookstore, outfitted with every possible type of whizbang technology now available to retailers. It had everything . . . except employees. It seems that in this age of information management, scanners, Radio Frequency Identification (RFID), "smart shelves," loyalty cards, and "pay passes," a store could be stocked, inventory could be tracked and reordered, and a customer could shop, all without traditional human labor.[1]

Exciting or frightening—or both? This chapter includes information about the growing use of technology in retail, as well as the laws and "rules of engagement" to be aware of when incorporating technology into the workplace. The focus here is *not* on how the technology *works*—other books and periodicals cover that in great detail—but on how it impacts the rights of employees and, in some cases, customers.

In addition, we'll briefly examine some current retail trends. Topics include

- In-store cameras
- Cellular phones on the job
- Identity checks and polygraph tests
- E-mail use and monitoring
- Hiring temporary workers
- Free speech and blogging
- Competing with e-commerce

Retail store owners have discovered that most of these issues require written company policies. Examples of how to word some of these policies are shared in this chapter.

## TECHNOLOGY AND WORKPLACE PRIVACY

As technology creates more and better ways to keep track of just about anything, serious debate has arisen over the lengths to which companies can go to monitor employees, both on and off the job. This debate has become part of employment contract and union negotiations, and sometimes ends up in court, in civil or even criminal lawsuits. The areas of the worker privacy debate most likely to be encountered by retail store managers include surveillance, drug testing, AIDS testing, background checks, and polygraph tests.

### In-store Cameras

Video surveillance is widely accepted in the retail workplace. In-store security cameras are part of robbery prevention in many stores, and they have the side benefit for management of possibly deterring other actions—credit card fraud, slip-and-fall or other workplace injury law-suits, and thefts by employees, to name a few. More than one-third of large and midsize companies say they use security cameras to monitor employees, and not all of the employees realize it. Today's video cameras are small, efficient, and easy to conceal.

The law does not limit companies in their use of video surveillance as long as they don't record sound, and there is usually no controversy when the cameras scan publicly accessible areas. But in areas of the store where employees or customers have a reasonable expectation of privacy (restrooms and changing rooms, for example), cameras may pose a legal problem for employers unless they can justify their business reasons for surveillance of otherwise private areas.[2] Since so many stores use security cameras, it is smart to think about the legal justification for any surveillance policy, making sure it is well documented and clear to all employees when they are hired.

## Computer and Telephone Monitoring

*Electronic surveillance* is probably the fastest-growing and most widely used form of employee surveillance because modern software makes it so easy to do. Employers use electronic surveillance to see how fast and effectively their computer-based employees work, how often they surf the Internet on company time, how long and to whom they talk on the telephone, even how fast and where they drive company-owned vehicles. Most of these surveillance areas are considered to be legally acceptable, but even here boundaries can blur and result in potential legal liability.

The **Omnibus Crime Control and Safe Streets Act of 1968**, for example, allows business phone calls to be monitored but forbids the monitoring of personal calls without prior employee consent. Companies that monitor workplace phone lines are legally required to "immediately" stop surveillance when a personal call is made, but there is no precise federal definition of a "personal" call or what time frame is considered "immediate." Further complicating this area is that many state laws prohibit *any* third-party telephone call monitoring and/or recording without the prior consent of all the monitored parties!

## Personal Calls at Work

With all this in mind, it's probably best to draft a policy about personal calls on the job and make it part of a new employee's orientation. The plethora of cellular phones makes this especially important, since it's

## THE RETAIL TELEPHONE ETIQUETTE ISSUE . . .

It's not a workplace privacy issue, but as long as we're on the subject of telephones, how often have you been frustrated by retail salesclerks who leave you standing at the checkout counter to answer a ringing phone, then proceed to have a lengthy conversation with the person on the other end of the line? You—who took the time to actually show up at the store—are left waiting, while the absent customer is attended to immediately, merely for having made the phone ring insistently.

The best suggestion for managers to make when training their sales team is to handle callers thusly: "I appreciate your taking the time to call, but I'm working with another customer right now. I'd be glad to take your name and number, though, and I can call you back as soon as I finish up with them. I hope that's all right. Thank you so much!"

In this manner, neither caller nor in-person shopper is being ignored; in fact, both are made to feel more important, by receiving the salesperson's undivided attention.

impossible for an employer to monitor an individual's personal cell phone. And, as high school kids prove daily in classrooms around the United States, when they can't *talk* on the phones, they can tap out instant messages on the keypads. The latest models can take photos and play computer games. In other words, the potential distractions from work are endless.

Private cell phone use has become a major workplace headache. Human resources consultant Toni C. Talbot suggests a stringent policy rather than a weak one, with language similar to this:[3]

> The use of personal cellular phones during work time will not be tolerated unless for emergency purposes. Employees may use personal cell phones during break periods, including meal breaks.

Some managers ask that employees turn their cell phones off altogether when they're on the job; others acknowledge that family members may have to get hold of employees during work hours and may occasionally call. The best policy is one that is strict enough to prevent persistent revisions and exceptions.

### E-mail and Internet Monitoring

iPods, BlackBerries, and other similar devices can be just as distracting as cell phones. The larger area of most concern to employers, however, is company computer use. In harassment claims, more workers are using e-mail and Internet-related problems as evidence, prompting some job sites to routinely monitor e-mail.

Although not all employees in retail are tied to computers, it is reasonable to assume that most have access to them and have the ability to send and receive e-mail. A 1998 survey by the American Management Association found that 27 percent of companies already monitored e-mail, an increase of 6.8 percent in just one year.[4] No doubt the percentage is even greater today, and it has resulted in an avalanche of debate about the propriety, legality, and overall effectiveness of monitoring employee computer use on the job.

Companies say the computers and Internet connections belong to them and they must monitor the output because they are legally liable for any improper or illegal content that comes from their equipment. Opponents argue that continual monitoring destroys the trust between worker and management and can actually reduce rather than increase productivity.

The fact is, employers have always monitored employee work habits: timing the keystrokes of data-entry clerks and typists, monitoring the length of bathroom and coffee breaks, listening in on phone calls to "check the quality of service," and seeing how long it takes delivery drivers to make their appointed rounds. In short, companies say they're doing what they always done; the only difference is the way the information is gathered.

Retailers are not all that interested in snooping in their employees' personal lives by reading e-mail messages, but they are not overstating the case that their liability can be major if there are problems with the company's Internet and e-mail systems. The following is a list of just a few key legal issues that are raised:

**Local liability** means the company is responsible for information disseminated by its systems. If an employee inadvertently or deliberately sends a virus along with an e-mail message from a company computer, the company is liable. If false information about competitors is sent out through the company system, the company is liable. And if sexually (or otherwise) harassing or intimidating e-mail messages are circulated, the company is liable if a harassment complaint is filed.

**Confidentiality breaches** include disclosure of trade secrets or other proprietary information. Sometimes it is accidental—a worker simply sends a document to the wrong address. Other times, it is a deliberate act of revenge by a disgruntled worker.

**Damages to standing and reputation** is the legal term when embarrassing e-mails are circulated, sometimes worldwide, with company logos or just the e-mail address revealing the point of origin.

**Lost productivity** is another big concern, simply because retailers aren't paying their accounting staff (for instance) to exchange jokes, photos, gossip, and recipes along with legitimate business. Overloading the network with nonwork surfing and e-mail messages (and the resultant spyware and "cookie" storage) is also a legitimate concern. Message and attachment storage takes up room, which costs money.

**Court-ordered e-mail retrieval** is a problem that is related to all the others. "E-mails are forever" is the catchphrase here, because they are essentially always accessible on storage media. Thus, whether it is a sexual harassment claim, wrongful termination lawsuit, industrial espionage case, libel against competitors, or other cause, courts often subpoena e-mail records as part of routine discovery (evidence-gathering) procedures.

The search itself is time-consuming and expensive for the company. Even more disastrous, the court sometimes orders company computer

## SEE YOU IN COURT? EMPLOYEE E-MAIL-RELATED CASES

In a 1999 Texas case, a Microsoft employee was suspended after allegations of sexual harassment and inventory questions—and was then denied full access to his e-mail files that he said would help with his defense. The employee sued Microsoft for invasion of privacy, because the company had accessed his password-protected personal folders and released the information to third parties. The employee compared it to searching a worker's locked locker. The court found that e-mails kept on the company computer were company property, regardless of password protection, and had been sent over a public network. It concluded that the company's interest in policing its e-mail system outweighed the employee's privacy interest.

This action followed a 1996 federal case in Pennsylvania, in which the court drew a similar conclusion in a wrongful termination lawsuit. The case involved an employee who sent e-mail from his home computer to a supervisor at his company. In those messages, he criticized company management and made threats against certain sales managers. When company officials saw the message, they checked all of the worker's e-mails, then fired him for "inappropriate and unprofessional comments" over the company e-mail system. The court found that the worker had no reasonable expectation of privacy with his company e-mails and could not claim wrongful termination on that basis.

*Source:* Barbara Weil Gall, "Company E-Mail and Internet Policies," on Web site GigaLaw.com, January 2000.

equipment to be seized as evidence pending the outcome of a case, which could be months or even years into the future.

Despite the disturbing "Big Brother" aspects of e-mail surveillance, it is fortunate for employers that the courts have generally found that employees cannot have a "reasonable expectation of privacy" when they are either writing e-mails on company computers or sending e-mails from their own computers to company computers.

As with sexual harassment and other touchy issues, a clearly stated and carefully defined "e-mail acceptable use policy" is important here. Its goal should be to clearly establish the precise level of privacy workers can expect in their e-mail, Internet, and general computer use while they are at work. This protects the company from claims of privacy violation, and sets boundaries to prevent conflicts. Many companies now require their outgoing messages on company computers to contain a standard disclaimer, stating that the privacy of the message cannot be guaranteed or giving instructions in case the message was received in error.

Some examples of policy statements include

- The computer, computer network, and all communications and transmission systems therein belong to the company, which reserves the right to inspect and monitor any and all communications and work product, at any and all times.
- The computer, computer network, and all communications and transmission systems therein are to be used for work-related data only (if the company wants to allow certain types or volumes of personal Web surfing or e-mails, specify that, too).
- The company may conduct occasional monitoring of system activity and/or individual use.
- Downloading or forwarding offensive e-mails, photos, Web sites, and other materials will result in disciplinary action and/or possible termination.
- Downloading software or opening EXE files from an outside sources without written system administrator permission is prohibited. *No exceptions.*
- Transmitting company information without written permission of [designated company official(s)] is prohibited. *No exceptions.*[5]

After a company creates its written policy, there are a variety of monitoring programs and software that track Internet and keyboard activity. Among them are iOpus STARR PRO, NET Observe, Spector Pro, and WinWhatWhere. Most of these programs can be installed secretly, but they can also include startup windows to remind workers that their every keystroke or Web click *may* be monitored.

## HOW CAREFUL SHOULD COMPANIES BE ABOUT THEIR ELECTRONIC COMMUNICATIONS?

We've seen e-mail messages which simply contain a line at bottom: "Remember, e-mail is not confidential." And then, in recent months we've seen these—the preachy, precautionary types of messages which are, perhaps, keeping corporate attorneys busy:

"The information contained in this electronic mail message, and any attachments thereto, is confidential and not intended to be distributed to third parties without the author's express written consent. By opening this e-mail, the recipient agrees not to disclose or forward to any third party, the content of the communication or any confidential or proprietary material attached to the communication, or otherwise submitted and identified by the sender."

"Regarding this e-mail and attachments: The e-mail is confidential and may contain privileged information. If you are not the intended recipient or receive it in error, you may not use, distribute, disclose or copy any of it (and such may be unlawful), and you must immediately notify and return it to us at (COMPANY ADDRESS) and destroy all copies. Views of individuals herein do not necessarily reflect those of (COMPANY NAME) or any of its subsidiaries. This e-mail does not constitute a binding offer, acceptance, amendment, waiver or other agreement, unless such intention is clearly stated in the e-mail. As good computing practice, you should conduct your own virus checking. Please note that we monitor, in accordance with applicable law, e-mails we receive."

From a senior management standpoint, a company must decide a few things about surveillance: how much monitoring they really need to do in the first place, whether they want to spend the money to upgrade systems, and how many hours are necessary to wade through all the data that it will generate. Perhaps it's better to hire employees who can be trusted in the first place. But read on . . .

## Identity Checks

In January 2005, law enforcement officials arrived at the Hewlett-Packard facility in Boise, Idaho, to arrest Daniel James Farinholt. The 44-year-old California child-molestation suspect had faked his own death in a boating accident in 2002 and had been living under an assumed name and working at the Boise plant for two years, as an employee of a temporary staffing agency used regularly by the plant.[6]

That kind of story sends chills down the spine of any business manager. How do you know your employees *are* who they say they are? Legally, what can be done to verify information given by job applicants?

Preemployment screening is on the rise, as discussed in Chapter 1, and the **Fair Credit Reporting Act** (FCRA) covers only those background checks done by third-party businesses that specialize in the collection of consumer information (credit reports, criminal records, etc.). Recently the FCRA was amended to allow "employee misconduct investigations" by third-party investigators without informing the employee in advance. This part of the law is known as the **Fair and Accurate Credit Transactions Act of 2003** (FACTA), and it applies when a worker is suspected of violating any government law or regulation (local, state, or federal), any preexisting written policies of their employer, or the rules of a self-regulatory organization.[7] Examples of the latter would be the Securities and Exchange Commission, in the case of a stockbroker, or a state liquor control commission, in the case of a store that sells alcohol.

The **Employee Polygraph Protection Act of 1988** (EPPA) prohibits most private-sector companies from subjecting employees to polygraph (lie detector) tests, especially during preemployment screening. It also bars employers from disciplining workers who refuse to take a polygraph, or asking about the results of any such test.

The EPPA does permit quite a few exceptions, such as randomly testing workers in investigations of economic losses or other business injuries. Retailers may be allowed to polygraph-test if their losses from shrinkage (theft) are significant enough for the company to make a successful legal argument for doing so. Companies that do national security-oriented business with the federal government are exempted altogether, and polygraph testing is permitted for all local, state, and federal government jobs.

## TEMPORARY WORKERS

One of the most profound workplace changes in the last 20 years has been the rise of part-time and temporary positions in retail. Stores have found that some very desirable groups of workers appreciate the flexibility of part-time scheduling, including students and parents of young families. Hiring part-timers and "temps" can also save money because their limited work hours do not qualify them for benefits, like health insurance and retirement accounts.

Temporary staffing employment agencies and professional employment organizations are known more commonly as "temp agencies" and PEOs. Both provide workers to a variety of businesses, but there are significant differences between them.

**Temp agencies** generally provide just that—temporary workers to cover for a permanent employee who is ill or on vacation, and to provide extra help during the busy seasons in retail. Temp jobs tend to last anywhere from a few days to several months.

The "temps" are employees of the agency and are basically rented to client employers at a rate that includes the temp's pay plus the agency's fees. The worker is paid by the temp agency, which also handles the administrative chores of withholding taxes from the person's paycheck. Some temp agencies also pay for or offer discounted health insurance and other benefits.

Despite anomalies like the identity fraud case in Boise mentioned earlier, temporary staffing is in many ways a good situation for companies and workers alike. Smart managers "audition" the temps as a way to see how well they would fit into the store as permanent employees. It's an effective way to minimize the chance of hiring the "wrong" people, then having to let them go. The same goes for the temp workers— they're checking out the store, too, for the same reasons of finding a "good fit." Temping also gives workers the chance to take as much time off as they want each year. And some companies use it as a way to avoid laying off full-time employees who may have been hired during a business upturn but who are not needed during a slowdown.[8]

The downside for temporary employees in retail is that there is not much chance for advancement, and temps are often hired to do the more mundane tasks, such as pricing and stocking shelves. An important thing for managers to remember is that temps are not aware of the many policies and procedures of the store—and it's your responsibility to brief them, or assign someone to do so. This includes basic job information, as well as some friendly advice on how to get along in your work environment.

**Professional employment organizations** (PEOs) differ from temp agencies because they not only provide workers for companies, they provide services and personnel to recruit, hire, and pay a group of employees to do certain administrative jobs for their client companies. They sign contracts to provide PEO service packages that cover a number of workers or positions, rather than individual contracts for each temp supplied to the company.

PEO workers are not temps, either; their terms of employment are permanent or open-ended rather than short-term with a specific ending date. And PEOs are considered "coemployers" with their client companies. They sell their service as a way for companies to "outsource" non-revenue-producing, back-office jobs like payroll, personnel management, tax compliance, and benefits.[9]

Hiring a PEO is a much bigger, more complex, and more long-term relationship with another company and its workers than contracts with temps and temp agencies, and PEOs vary widely in the worker types they provide and the manner in which they manage and take care of their employees.

For managers, the most critical legal consideration when using part-time or temporary workers hired through an outside agency is the ability to prove (if necessary) that your company is not trying to bypass paying legitimate benefits to employees by hiring and paying them as contract workers. In March 2005, for example, 33 temporary workers sued Hewlett-Packard Company, claiming they have been shortchanged on benefits. Their complaint refers to them as "common-law employees," entitled to all the benefits of employee status—including health insurance, employee stock options, pension plans, holidays, sick leave, and paid vacation. The suit was filed in U.S. District Court on behalf of 3,000 workers hired by temp agencies. The Internal Revenue Service uses a list of 20 criteria to help employers determine if a worker is an employee or a contractor.[10]

## FREE SPEECH AND BLOGGING

The last couple of U.S. presidential elections have proven that politics can still be lively. They have also proven that the nation is sharply divided along political party lines. This debate is likely to continue, and to spill over occasionally into the workplace as people get to know one another's views and opinions. Retailers and their managers are not immune from this trend. How do you think Democratic workers feel when their store owner is seen at the city's high-dollar Republican fund-raiser, or is named in the newspaper as a major contributor to GOP campaigns?

Free speech has long been a workplace issue. The U.S. Constitution's First Amendment affirms the right of citizens to speak freely on almost any subject. Of course, limits have been adjudicated with regard to yelling "Fire!" in crowded theaters or threatening others with physical harm, but almost anything else goes—outside the workplace. But inside the workplace, private employers can regulate free speech as they see fit. As long as they are not discriminating or retaliating against anyone for union organizing, they don't have to worry too much about running afoul of the First Amendment.

However, certain types of free speech (such as complaints) are protected—even if the company objects or prohibits them—if the topic is a matter of "public concern." For example, complaints about improperly stored materials or other safety issues, or about a company doing something illegal, are usually protected. People also cannot be disciplined for refusing to work for, or contribute to, political candidates or causes. On the other hand, griping publicly about pay rates, layoffs, or other company issues that are not normally matters of public concern would not be protected.

Workers are also protected if they decline to salute the flag, say the Pledge of Allegiance, or participate in company prayers. However, they cannot refuse to wear company logos and/or uniforms while at work. As you can imagine, all of this gets complicated in cases where a worker's personal grievance or problem touches on larger issues, like sexual harassment or invasions of privacy.[11]

Where technology comes into the free speech debate is in the area of Web logs, or "blogs"—personal Internet Web sites where individuals hold forth on many subjects involving politics, society, and technology—and their jobs. It is estimated that 27 percent of U.S. adults online read blogs, and 7 percent write them regularly.[12] There are Web sites that actually invite employees (and customers) of various major retail chains to share their negative experiences with the world online.

The problem is, most "bloggers" are not professional writers or journalists and don't know even the basic laws about libel, slander, confidentiality, and trademark laws that govern publishing, whether on the printed page or the Internet.[13]

Companies throughout the U.S. have disciplined or fired current employees who write too revealingly or critically about their jobs—and threatened former employees who did the same. So whether or not a company approves of employee blogging, a key way to avoid misunderstandings is to have an established, written "blog policy" that workers understand and sign as a condition of employment.

## COMPETING WITH E-COMMERCE

It is true that consumers are doing more of their shopping online. It is also true that online shopping has its downsides, and that not all Internet-based marketing efforts succeed. Online fraud is described as "rampant," with the U.S. Federal Trade Commission logging more than 100,000 Internet-related transaction complaints for 2002 (totaling $15 million; up from $6 million in 2001), and the National Fraud Information Center reporting 37,183 complaints in 2003. Average losses per online consumer have also climbed—from $468 in 2002, to $527 in 2003, to $803 in 2004.[14,15]

Even customers who are comfortable with technology resent the constant onslaught of adware, spam, spyware, and phishing (messages from scammers posing as banks and credit card companies, asking you to "verify" account information—so they can steal it). Merchants are doing more to shield themselves from fraudulent practices, but this often doesn't help the consumer, who is left fighting the identity fraud or bogus credit card charge and having to reclaim or rebuild his or her own credit history.

The experts insist there will always be a place for traditional "brick-and-mortar" stores—at least, for those that continue to keep things interesting by developing new concepts and training employees to provide excellent levels of service and meet customers' needs for speed, choice, and convenience. Add to this the desire for human contact, and the social activism of many who choose to patronize the smaller, locally owned stores in their communities rather than the more imposing superstores, and you've got a loyal customer base if you can figure out how to impress them. (Let's presume that is one reason you are reading this book.)

Conventional department stores are currently having to undergo the most radical reinventions. In 2004, their average sales grew only 2.5 percent. (An exception was Neiman Marcus, where service has long been a top priority and sales were up 10.6 percent in 2004). However, compare department stores as a category to fast-growing specialty stores, and it is obvious that the smaller, specialty formats are hot. Even the giant discounters like Wal-Mart no longer enjoy double-digit growth; that category's sales actually fell slightly from 2002 to 2004.[16]

Speaking of giants, perhaps one of the problems in retail is that there is so much of it—nearly 20 feet of store space per capita in the United States, compared to 8 feet per capita in the 1970s. The superstore trend is not just overwhelming for some time-crunched shoppers; bigger stores mean bigger expenses, and it is difficult for sales to keep up with them.

## Learning from Winning Retail Concepts

During the first few years of this new century, a number of retailers have been in the business spotlight for their innovative concepts or approaches. As a fitting end to this chapter, they're listed here alphabetically. The notes about what they've done that is fresh, trendsetting, and encouraging for the retail scene overall are reprinted with the permission of their sources: major retail research and consulting firms Kurt Salmon Associates (New York and Atlanta), and McMillan|Doolittle (Chicago).[17]

- **American Girl.** This company sells so much more than dolls and accessories. The real deal is the event and adventure that is created in the American Girl store. Little girls (with paying adults in tow) can take their dolls (or buy a new one) to the doll hair salon or to tea in the American Girl Café. No trip to the American Girl store in New York City would be complete without tickets to the American Girl Revue, a stage production based on stories from the American Girl storybook collection. And, of course, little girls will want to dress in matching American Girl outfits to attend the show. It's no wonder the company experienced a third-quarter (2004) sales increase of 18 percent, bringing sales to $49 million (Kurt Salmon Associates).

- **Build-A-Bear Workshop®.** This is one of the best-executed retail concepts we've seen in many years. The attention to detail and to the target customer is brilliant. For those unfamiliar with the store, Build-A-Bear allows children to create their own teddy bears. A customer chooses a bearskin from 20 varieties, then takes it to a filling station and watches it get stuffed. A customer can customize the bear in many ways—from sounds it will make to its wardrobe and name. Customers can even fill out adoption papers! The experience and the store are thrilling for both children and parents. In addition to being an astute retailer that manages to smoothly blend creating an experience and selling products, Build-A-Bear incorporates two powerful concepts that are becoming big factors in tomorrow's hot ideas: (1) *generational targeting* (focusing on a very specific audience) and (2) *personalization* (the ability to create a product that can be made to the customer's exact specifications) (McMillan|Doolittle).

- **The Container Store.** One of its core business philosophies is that three *good* people equal one *great* person in terms of business productivity. So why not hire only great people? The Container Store's philosophy about employee development sets it apart from other retailers. It places so much importance on service that every first-year, full-time salesperson receives about 240 hours of training—in an industry where the average is about eight hours—and training continues throughout an employee's career. Salespeople do not work on commission; instead, they're either salaried or paid by the hour with wages far above the retail industry norm. The justification for this expense is loyalty (Kurt Salmon Associates).

- **The Gap.** The Gap, of course, is no slouch at brand extension. It's had tremendous success with Gap Kids and Gap Baby and is still spinning its wheels with the new Gap Body, which specializes in underwear. Gap followed demographic shifts when it converted Banana Republic into a fashion-forward store for its older customers and when it created Old Navy to be a discount Gap that also appealed to Gap's younger customers (McMillan|Doolittle). (*Author's note:* 2005 brings yet another Gap concept, aimed at clothing women ages 35 and older.)
- **The Limited.** This company has been a master of creating new formats based on either product demand or demographic opportunity. Limited Too targets the hot preteen segment. Bath & Body Works and Victoria's Secret were both Limited spinoffs. Now, Bath & Body has launched a concept called White Barn Candle Company that targets the growth in home accessories. Abercrombie & Fitch, another Limited re-creation, has been hot with the critical teen and Generation X segments. It is rolling out Abercrombie, also targeting the preteen market, and has a concept called Hollister that is slightly more casual and offers lower prices than its current positioning (McMillan|Doolittle).
- **PETsMART.** Not all investment in employees must involve spending money. PETsMART, for example, discovered it would learn more about job candidates if it moved interviews from the back offices to the sales floor, where they could be observed relating to "pet parents." PETsMART executives also spend a week working in stores in an effort to remain focused on the consumer (Kurt Salmon Associates).
- **Sephora.** The French-originated cosmetics concept represents the antithesis of the department store cosmetics and perfume-buying experience. The store design is visually spectacular, letting customers know that they are going to be experiencing something very different. The product is not behind glass cases; it is available for customers to hold and test. Sephora groups products alphabetically, broken out of the traditional brand categories. Salespeople are available, and they have tremendous product knowledge, but they design the experience to offer customers the option of self-service or service, rather than a traditional service mode. Selections are enormous: There are lots of choices for consumers, which is another critical aspect of control. Sephora's concept is also scalable—it works in smaller mall stores and in large freestanding flagship stores. The brand is growing and becoming synonymous with beauty (McMillan|Doolittle).

If this list of concepts could be summarized, retailers can learn that attention to highly targeted markets—making shopping fun and interesting, even if it's quick . . . making employees a top priority . . . and commitment to providing outstanding service—all are necessary for success today. The consulting firms that selected these winning retailers acknowledge it is not easy to stand out from the crowd in retail, but it can be done. To their own clients, they suggest the following starting points on which to build interest and excitement:

- **Challenge the store environment.** Make things different, more holistic, more special. Make shopping enjoyable for the customer.
- **Intensify service.** Think about what you can add before, during, and after the sale, in terms of product, environment, and services.
- **Let the customer control the process.** Make sure there are plenty of choices, and that the shopping experience is not frustrating or intimidating.
- **Save customers' time.** Brainstorm ways to make the experience faster and easier. Find methods to "bundle" (combine) products with related services.
- **Watch consumer trends.** At the moment, hot trends include ethnic influences, home accessories (for folks who can't afford to move or remodel but want an updated look), and stores that target teen lifestyles.

Perhaps the best thing about these ideas is that they benefit employees and customers as well as paying off in terms of sales. If managers can keep a store vibrant, relevant, and fun, the best employees will want to work there, and the customers will visit regularly—and tell their friends about their experiences. With all that going on, who'd want to stay home and shop online?

## CHAPTER SUMMARY

Technology now impacts almost every aspect of retail store operation. This chapter summarized the major challenges and policies managers must familiarize themselves with to use technology without infringing on the rights of employees and, in some cases, customers.

Video surveillance is used for a number of good reasons, and it is permitted in retail as long as sound is not recorded and in areas that are in public view. Video is not permitted in other parts of a store—including dressing rooms, employee locker rooms, and restrooms—unless management can prove a business reason (a significant increase in shrinkage, for example) that would justify the use of cameras.

The prevalence of cellular phone use was discussed in this chapter, with guidelines for employees' personal phone use on work time. The store's phone lines can be monitored, and so can e-mail messages. The point is not that retailers want to micromanage their workers' communication, but that companies have serious legal liability on multiple fronts, from harassment claims to confidentiality breaches to computer viruses that impact their network. Companies also have a reasonable expectation that employees actually *work* when they're on the job instead of spending time surfing the Internet and exchanging personal messages with friends.

Even the hiring process is impacted by technology, in the use of pre-screening investigations for background checks of job candidates. The guidelines for polygraph testing are also mentioned.

Trends covered in this chapter included the use of temporary workers and contract workers through professional employment organizations (PEOs) and "free speech" issues in the workplace, including employees blogging about jobs on Internet Web sites. The chapter ended with a look at the challenges retailers face to compete with e-commerce and summarized the innovative concepts of seven retail companies to give students ideas of what "works" when customer service and employee satisfaction are management priorities.

## DISCUSSION QUESTIONS

1. Write a policy for receiving and making personal phone calls on a retail sales job, and justify it to your class, both on practical and legal grounds.
2. What is "a reasonable expectation of privacy," and how does this concept affect the way a company secures its computer systems? Do you think the rules should change if the retailer is undergoing a serious theft problem?
3. What should a manager consider when planning a combination of full-time, part-time, and temporary workers?
4. What do you think a company *should not* allow employees to say, on or off the job, when they are blogging? Be specific.
5. Who do you think will "win" in the retail wars: traditional merchants or e-commerce? Briefly explain your reasoning.

# ENDNOTES

1. Glenn Law, "NRF Expo Gives Glimpse of Retail's Future," *National Jeweler* magazine, March 1, 2005.
2. Denise Kersten, "Privacy Protections at Work Are Few and Far Between," *USA Today*, November 7, 2002.
3. Toni C. Talbot, General Partner, HRMS, LLC, "Cell Phones in the Workplace," *Michigan Forward* magazine, May 2003.
4. Barbara Weil Gall, "Company E-mail and Internet Policies," on Web site GigaLaw.com, January 2000.
5. Web site email-policy.com, 2004.
6. The *Idaho Statesman*, January 19, 2005.
7. *Fact Sheet 16: Employment Background Checks*, Privacy Rights Clearinghouse, San Diego, California, June 2004.
8. J. Steven Niznik, "Temping for a Living: Are Temp Agencies and Jobs Right for You?" Jobsearch on Web site About.com, PRIMEDIA, Inc., New York.
9. "Definition of a Professional Employment Organization," Compensation Solutions, Inc., Oakland, New Jersey.
10. Bill Roberts, "33 People File Suit for Employee Benefits from HP," The *Idaho Statesman*, March 22, 2005.
11. Duncan J. Forsyth, attorney, Halloran & Sage, LLP, "Free Speech: Constitutional Protections in the Workplace," *Connecticut Employment Law Letter*, Hartford, Connecticut, December 2000.
12. Anick Jesdadun, "Blog-Related Firings Prompt Calls for Clearer Company Policies," Associated Press, reprinted in *Idaho Statesman*, March 5, 2005.
13. Jennifer Balderama, "Free Speech, Virtually: Legal Constraints on Web Journals Surprise Many 'Bloggers,'" *Washington Post*, December 18, 2002.
14. Thomas Claburn, "Online Merchants Fight the Good Fight Against Fraud," *Information Week*, November 22, 2004.
15. Jennifer Mulrean, "Protect Yourself: The Safest Ways to Pay Online," on Web site of MSN Money, moneycentral.com, 2003.
16. Katherine Reynolds Lewis, "Changing Consumer Habits Drive a Retail Revolution," ©Newhouse News Service, Washington, D.C., February 28, 2005.
17. The descriptions of Build-A-Bear Workshop® and The Gap were quoted from the book *Winning at Retail: Developing a Sustained Model for Retail Success* by Willard N. Ander and Neil Z. Stern, Senior Partners with McMillan|Doolittle (New York: John Wiley & Sons, ©2004), and used with permission of the authors.

# GLOSSARY

**B**

**blog**   Slang for Web log, an individual's personal thoughts and opinions posted on an Internet Web site to be shared publicly with anyone who reads it.

**blogger**   A person who writes a Web log.

**blogging**   The act of writing a Web log.

**brick-and-mortar**   Retail industry jargon for a store's physical site or building.

**bundle**   Merchant's jargon for combining products with related services to prompt a larger sale. The practice is known as *bundling*.

**business agent**   A local labor union employee who serves as contract administrator and handles compliance, grievance, and union-company relationships with a variety of work sites in a geographic area.

**C**

**cafeteria-style benefits**   A benefit plan in which an employer assigns each worker a dollar amount to be used for benefits (insurance, child care, and so on), and offers a list of benefits from which workers can select based on their own needs.

**cash balance plan**   A type of retirement account in which the employer contributes a defined amount each year, based on worker income and seniority, and guarantees the account will grow annually by a fixed percentage. When workers reach retirement age, they generally have the option of taking the final amount, as either an annuity or a lump sum.

**collective bargaining**   A labor union's negotiations for similar pay and benefits for its member workers doing similar jobs, regardless of the industry, company, and/or region in which they work.

**compensation benefits**  Employee benefits that have a measurable financial cost and worth, such as health insurance, a retirement or pension plan, and paid vacation time.

**craft union**  A labor union for craftspeople of a particular skill or trade, such as electricians, machinists, and plumbers.

## D

**defined benefit plan**  A traditional pension plan, in which a specified benefit amount and duration is financed entirely by employer contributions and is paid according to employee longevity and earnings formulas. Abbreviated *DB.*

**defined contribution package**  Currently the more popular type of retirement plan, it is usually financed as a combination of employer and employee contributions; it generally gives the employee more control over how the money is invested, and it is transferable if the employee changes jobs. Abbreviated *DC.*

**disability insurance**  An insurance policy that provides income to a person in case of an accident or injury that curtails his or her ability to work.

## E

**electronic surveillance**  The use of technology to monitor employees' work habits (how fast they type, how often they surf the Internet on company time, how long and to whom they talk on the telephone, and so on).

## F

**fit-for-duty testing**  See *impairment testing.*

**flextime**  A work schedule that allows options for flexible starting and ending hours, compressed work schedules (more hours per day, but fewer days per week on the job), and job sharing (when one or more employees "share" hours to create a single, full-time work presence).

## G

**grievance**  A complaint filed by a labor union member against a company that alleges a violation of the terms of the union contract in effect at the company, or alleges a violation of civil or criminal law.

**grievant**  A person who files a grievance.

**Guaranteed Income Stream**  A benefit plan that guarantees certain percentages of income until retirement for senior workers in heavily unionized industries that experience large industry-related layoffs. Abbreviated *GIS.*

## H

**hostile environment sexual harassment**  A condition in which sexual advances or behavior create an intimidating work environment that interferes with an employee's job performance.

# I

**impairment testing**   A test that measures an employee's readiness to perform certain tasks when he or she reports to the workplace, including vision, hand-eye coordination, reasoning ability, and reaction time. Abbreviated *IT.*

**individual retirement account**   A tax-deferred savings account earmarked as a person's retirement income. Abbreviated *IRA.*

**industrial union**   A labor union made up of all employees in a particular industry, such as hotel workers or textile workers.

# K

**Keogh account**   A tax-deferred retirement savings account for a self-employed person, funded by that individual instead of by an employer.

# L

**leave bank**   A system to keep track of employees' accumulated time off. Workers can "save" their sick leave or vacation time and use it as needed.

# M

**mismatch letter**   A notice from the Social Security Administration advising an employer that they have reported a particular Social Security number that doesn't match what the SSA has on file for an employee.

# N

**negligent hiring**   The basis for a lawsuit against an employer when an employee's actions hurt others through injury, a crime, sexual harassment, or another, equally serious problem.

# O

**off-the-clock work**   The illegal practice of asking or requiring hourly employees to work unpaid hours by starting work before they "clock in," or continuing to work after they "clock out."

# P

**professional employment organization**   A company that contracts with other companies to recruit, hire, and pay administrative workers for its client companies. Abbreviated *PEO.*

# Q

**quid pro quo sexual harassment**   Sexual advances or behavior by a higher-ranking worker or manager that are used as a condition of employment or to make job-related decisions (demotion, promotion, and so on) based on the employee's reaction to the harassment. The Latin term *quid pro quo* means "something for something," one thing in return for another.

**R**

**reimbursement account**   A type of employee benefits plan that allows a certain amount of each worker's pretax income to be used to purchase various health and family-based benefits.

**S**

**sexual harassment**   A type of discrimination, generally defined as unwanted sexually oriented verbal or physical behavior that focuses on a person's gender and makes that person feel uncomfortable or intimidated.

**shift differential**   An extra amount of hourly pay for employees who work less desirable shifts, such as late-night or overnight shifts.

**shop steward**   A person who is an employee of a company and also serves as that company's labor union representative for employees who are union members.

**Supplemental Unemployment Benefits**   An income maintenance plan for union workers that guarantees an income for a number of months after a layoff. Abbreviated *SUBs*.

**T**

**task analysis**   Listing a worker's responsibilities and tasks for a particular job—the purpose of the task, how it is done, and what skills and equipment are needed to do it—to prepare a written job description.

**third-party sexual harassment**   The type of lawsuit or claim filed by workers who are not the specific targets of sexual harassment, objecting to such behavior because of its overall impact on them or their workplace.

**U**

**unemployment compensation**   A program funded jointly by employers and the U.S. government that provides partial pay for up to 26 weeks to workers who have been laid off while they actively search for a new job.

**W**

**workers' compensation**   An insurance program funded jointly by employers and the U.S. government that makes payments to employees who can't work after being injured on the job. "Workers' comp" policies are administered by state insurance commissions.

**workplace benefits**   Employee benefits that focus on work-life balance, comfort, or compensation other than money, such as flextime, an employee fitness center, and reserved parking.

**wrongful discharge**   A terminated employee's legal claim that he or she was dismissed from a job without good or sufficient legal reason for the termination, or in violation of a law or contract.

# INDEX